MY SIDE OF THE TABLE

Memoirs of an Intuitive Healer

SEERA WOLF

My Side of the Table:
Memoirs of an Intuitive Healer
First Edition

© 2015 Karen L. Pringle
All rights reserved.

ISBN 978-1-329-18248-6

Cover Design and Editing by
Jennifer Soldner
http://jennifersoldner.com

To my Great, Great Grandfather Stephenson,
my Ancestor.
His blood runs in my veins.
His words I have heard.

Mud in the Water

I began the summer of 2002 in Santa Cruz, California with the devastating news that I had yet again lost my rental housing. In that area, the market is expensive and difficult to find another place, especially when you had planned to stay around for a while.

I searched and searched and couldn't find a thing. Even with friends' assistance, no one could find anything. I wasn't willing to part with our rescue pit bull puppy Amber nor our cat Coco, so I took a leap of faith and contacted family who had previously relocated to Northern Minnesota. I was longing to have a nest, a solid foundation in which to raise my son.

With the move came the harsh loneliness of leaving behind all the friends I held dear back in Santa Cruz. That loneliness is only amplified by the long, bitter Northern winters. Snow, cold, ice; elements in which I'd never lived nor driven, but I was courageous. I stayed positive and pushed through all the while thinking, *No problem, I can do that!*

I spent just about everything I had to get the move accomplished and reduced quite a bit of our furniture, leaving some to be shipped with us while I drove our little city car, a Jetta, across the country with my son, who was six years of age at that time, our dog and cat, making it a fun and extended journey.

The last state, where we stopped for gas was North Dakota. My son was so young and I was very protective. As I pumped the gas in Fargo, a man, clearly spotting the *U-Haul* trailer hitched to our bumper, asked where we were headed.

"Minnesota," I replied.

"Oh no," he scoffed. "The people there are really weird! They are really different…especially for you, coming from…" The man leaned far over the pump, trying to catch a glimpse of our license plate. "Your plate says California."

I noted what he had to say and thought to myself, *maybe he has just had some poor experiences with Minnesotans and, mine will certainly be different!* I was determined to remain positive about making this move work out. I was ready for a new journey.

But, held deep in my heart echoed the words of an old friend, Evelyn. Though I am not so sure she called herself one, Evelyn was what we call a Shaman. The title of Shaman is one that carries with it a lot of weight and as we head into this journey I am going to show you precisely what that means.

Evelyn, a beautiful woman of forty with dirty blonde hair, she lived right near the Pacific Ocean in Santa Cruz. Whenever I think of her, I am transported back to her yurt. She helped me in many ways to prepare the way ahead for this journey. I would visit her home and work together in her yurt. I am not even sure now how we had come to this, but she had a really wonderful space in her backyard with skins and drums and a massage table where I would often lay. As we spent many hours discussing my move to the north, it helped me to prepare. We talked about important things related with my ancestors and certain events of my life and, at times, powerful work and feelings were evoked through our chats. There were times I recall when the feelings were so powerful, I would physically shake as I sobbed. During these moments, Evelyn and I would work together with a hawk feather and at times, used pictures of my ancestors. We processed many emotions and energies in preparation for this forthcoming journey.

During one of our meetings, she said something to me I will never forget. She stated, "You are stepping into a very hard journey, one of your ancestors and you will be challenged greatly."

Others that I knew through my attendance at the American School of Herbalism where I would bring my son along would tell me, "go! Be a light seed. You know much and you will open many eyes!"

As I reflect upon that time now, the feeling is similar to learning you are pregnant with your first child and you are excited though you do not know exactly what is coming your way. You can seek guidance, but none can tell you exactly what you will experience.

Just recently, I visited with a client at a coffee shop for a half an hour Guidance session and I used similar words. I told her, "You will have several changes that take you from your comfort zone in the near future." It is not for me to illustrate these events completely as that would take away the free will and self-enterprise, which I would never do.. Guidance is just that, a hand to hold onto, as a person who has ventured a bit further perhaps down the river.

After we got onto the road and processed the feelings of leaving our home in Santa Cruz, California, the place of which I will always hold dear, we really began to enjoy the cross country trip, stopping at various places.

There is nothing better than seeing the country on a road trip with a young child who has a fresh perspective. Stopping to play and just feeling the earth by having our bare feet on new soil each day. Being cut free from the responsibilities of the home and job, and completely at one with the trip and the family was a dream. My dream.

And my dream come true. I always wanted to live in a full time recreational vehicle. A "bus," as some call it. All of my friends knew that one day I was going to just live a blissful nomadic life.

My son and I also ventured into a small town, where my father was staying in Idaho, at some dorms where he was temporarily escaping the summer heat of Arizona. In Minnesota people "snowbird" away to warmer climates in the harsh winters and many in Arizona often get out of the intense heat in the summers. A local woman was admiring our dog, Amber, while we were in town. My father talked me into re-homing Amber to this lovely lady who was really smitten with her and owned a large farm with lovely children. Many times, over the next few years, I spoke with her and Amber really loved her new life and, to be honest, as much as I missed her dearly, it was not entirely fair that I was unsure of where we would land. Giving some of our initial hardships getting settled in Minnesota, looking back, perhaps Amber's new home was for the best.

We arrived to the small town of Cloquet, Minnesota in early July. I can replay the scene, the feelings, in my mind like a movie. The sun was shining brightly overhead, it was warm and the countryside was just beautiful. It was great timing to get off the road for a bit and greet the family.

I had a very small budget to help me get reestablished in our new location and had a plan to rent an apartment in Minnetonka that was really lovely. A school there was affiliated with my son's school from Santa Cruz and I had a law firm referral to a couple of the firms with which I had been speaking before departing Santa Cruz. I had worked at a lovely firm that treated its employees very well. I made pretty good money, but with raising a child in a very expensive area, it is hard to save or purchase a home.

But Zahwa, my son, was young and wanted to be near his cousin, so plans aside, we decided to stay in Cloquet. I really could have given more thought to the difficulties of finding work in such a small town, but I managed to find a few part time jobs, albeit not very quickly.

I needed to get some food support as our finances dwindled quickly and I had a young child. The budget was not comfortable. I had my massage therapy practitioner credential but was far too intimidated to actually parlay that into a business in California. I gave a few massages here and there but was really shaky. Still, I knew that I probably could do well.

And thus, we were now committed to Cloquet. I quickly began to wonder if I had made the right decision.

Coming from Santa Cruz, California, and being very intuitive and interested in energy work, doing a lot of study into natural healing, and all the things I had experienced, including travel to other parts of the world to meditate on the ruins and such, made it really hard to come to a place where people in large part did not really understand "energy work."

At the time, the United States was becoming really focused on the situation in Iraq and that had really put a negative spin on finding work. People in smaller cities and towns tightened their belts more quickly, it seems. What was available was Wal-Mart and an evening shift, which was not something I felt willing to do as it required leaving my son with strangers in the evening. This was far outside of my maternal comfort zone. Moving somewhere with a child and not having a support system of any kind is really disorienting.

And so, I decided it was time to try my hand at a massage business. Winter was coming and the cold was biting. I had never experienced something like this before. But I was very thankful with how our lives were moving forward. That is, until a therapist who was renting another room in our building began to feel uncomfortable after hearing me make the statement, "I like her energy." Something so simple and suddenly our rental agreement was an issue.

I had already gone to the city offices to pay my $100 in order to have an FBI background check to become licensed. So holding onto our rental agreement was a must.

At the time, I wondered, *how do we learn to overcome that resistance to deal directly with conflict, or perceived conflict?* Truth be told, whenever you are pushed or in a corner, the advocate inside yourself will arise. I had to deal with this conflict head on. I met with the other renter in person, nicely saying that if I should do anything that warranted my being dismissed that we could and should talk about it as grown women face to face versus leaving a message on my home answering machine.

With the worry of our rental agreement now behind us, I tediously grew my massage business day after day, networking in a town where I knew nobody. The move and the new business venture along with the growing sense of loneliness left me dealing with some really deep depression and anxiety. I was in fear, I was not eating as I knew was best for us, and my son was struggling in his new school.

My business increased a bit at a time, I worked a regular job part time and then also would work a client in the evening after they finished their job, until I grew it from the discount rate of $35 per hour to $75 per hour having become known and respected.

I realize you will never make everyone happy in terms of how you are perceived. How I view food, living, the world and our responsibilities, as well as my energy work and intuition is not going to mesh well with those from a small town.

At times, I honestly thought I would be burned at the stake. I had ladies tell me that their church groups believed I was working with the devil. I was horrified that people initially behaved that way. I cried buckets of tears and overpaid my dues.

But despite the perceptions of some in town, I offered the locals the best massage ever. Esalen style, fluid, with top notch energy work, warm stones, essential oils, and the best oils in a warm clean room, always on time. I moved their energy and I guided them with natural healing. Often times, I was able to give them the names of their ancestors, medically intuitive information, and much more.

You see, I have developed my sense of 'sight' from the time I was a young girl, making me very advanced compared to those who began their interest as adults in many ways. I was born a Shaman, a Seer, a Healer. I worked through my apprenticeship for free and nearly free, earning my reputation, studying for the last thirty years in natural health and healing, herbs, Ayurveda, spirituality, and observation of nature.

As I would read books to my son during the winters, about the Wendigo and others by local authors, I began to understand Minnesota a little better. I learned to see its beauty in the ice and snow, the glory of the hawks elegantly gliding over Hawk Ridge, learning to communicate with the nature I had never before known.

I learned to welcome the snow, the ice, the cold. I learned to give thanks for the eagles above me and for Lake Superior, the "Cold Mother" who has taught many so much.

I had to learn to walk with Northern Node, the Elder. And, I had to learn to navigate the Earth Element that echoed very strong through the Minnesotan land. I was very etheric and I also related myself as a very strong Water Element. The west, my Californian home, was all about water. Moving to Northern Minnesota combined my strong water element with an earth element and that made *mud*.

It is difficult to see clearly and regulate one's emotions or feel balanced when you are engulfed in mud.

But currently, I live a mile from an Indian Reservation called Fond Du Lac and I am fortunate to be so close to the indigenous Ojibwe peoples. I do my best to show that there are easier ways to live and more natural modes to treating disease. I respect all and have walked a long path and learned much. I will always continue to learn. These aspects have helped me learn ways to clear my mind, to clear away the mud.

All of my life, the Wolf has been my sacred animal, caring for me as a young girl and showing up in times of need. Teaching me to posture, sense, feel and smell like a wolf. Teaching me loyalty and tender secrets.

What was so foreign here was that the Midwest, and especially the far upper North Midwest, was seemingly still about twenty years behind what I was experiencing in Santa Cruz. It was like going back in time. There were moments when I was extremely frustrated by this and I still can be.

Living in this small town has taught me that there are aspects of this life with which many are unfamiliar. Many have come into my massage office and completed the health history, confused by the section where it asks whether they are interested in "Shamanic works." They ask me to explain as many are unfamiliar with what that means.

It is for this reason that I feel a strong pull to share with you my side. To show you what it means to be born a Shaman. These stories I wish to share with you are merely the surface of what lies beneath. They are but a glimpse into the life of a Seer. They are my works in part of the nearly thirteen years of practice in Cloquet, Minnesota.

In these pages, I wish to welcome you to my side of the table.

WHAT IS A SHAMAN

Not everyone knows what a Shaman is, does, or what kind of services we bring to life, for the people, planet, and animals.

Not everybody knows what Ancestor work is. Long before things were as we know today, we celebrated our ancestors. They are our family and they are a part of us, in our hearts and spirits.

Shamans have developed ourselves and shaped our clay, as we knew this was our role from a very young age. We were passionate about taking care of the planet, caring for the young, the infants and the elderly. We were always observing, noticing how healing occurs. We love plants, and walking the earth, observing, and we have learned a sense of deep patience on our river of life.

We are aware of and link with all the elements: Fire, Water, Air, Earth, and Akasha (spirit). While this may sound like many other systems, it is a fact of life. We breathe air and it is vital. As I have enjoyed yoga over the decades and am currently training as a yoga instructor, I am fascinated by the art of breath. Even on the great megaliths, the great pyramids, you see hieroglyphs which illustrate how important the breath is and it is what we focus on, as relaxed breathing takes the brain into an Alpha state; a relaxed meditative state which is healing.

We rely on digestive fire to aid us in processing our food into nutrients and in Ayurveda it is spoken about maintaining that digestive fire and how to keep it strong.

Earth is supporting, and provides a basis for us all to live, and water nourishes and yet is also a strong force. We must have water to survive in our physical bodies.

I deeply care that people treat this beautiful planet well, it is our home.

I began exercises like billet Reading in the 1960s, animal communication with monkeys, large birds, large dogs, and more in the 1960s forward. I would sit and write poetry and I was very quiet, and very introverted in my younger days.

I had often heard the Ancestors which became more prominent to me at age 15. Like everybody else, I, too, had all the physical lessons to learn: privilege, entitlement, self-discipline, partners, health, food issues, learning to prepare food, and navigate this ability to work with energy.

I made a lot of mistakes, just as all people do. I had wounds that I had to learn to deal with – and I learned from them.

Along with everyday life, I had to cope with the additional layer that came from being unusually intuitive. It scared people, especially those closest to me. As an adolescent, it is common to begin to feel a sense of "other." Or, with that developmental stage, to wonder, *why am I different?* It was not the "cool" status it is quite at this time.

I have made the mistakes of using my power inappropriately when I was younger.

I've become familiar with the wide range of emotions: anger, rage, grief, loss, and lonely feelings beyond belief.

But a Shaman's purpose, the reason for all the struggles and learning I have endured through the years, is to provide Guidance. Guidance from our world experiences, our spirit experiences, and our own natural desires.

I had a strong desire to learn of natural healing for the last three decades, topics like:

- Making food your medicine.
- Using supplements when necessary and knowing which ones to use.
- Learning how to truly nourish our companions (canines) by feeding them their ancestral diet, giving them proper exercise and so forth.

When I meet with a client in a Shamanic Guidance session, I initially look at their face, hand, and tongue readings. I gather an overall energy or a picture.

I hear what is happening with a brief share. I want to find the root gradually if there is imbalance, or really hear what would balance the person.

These could be things such as:

- Their home life; partner, job, business, relocation, children.

- Their lack of self-love or self-esteem.

- Their business is ready to launch or failing or not producing income.

- Their partner: struggles, issues of trust, respect.

- Sometimes, and often, it is a woman who is struggling with infertility and if she is completely committed, I can help her to get results to the best of my ability.

Every single disease begins in the mind. For this reason, I do what I call the "Wellness Consultation" which includes MindBody, food as medicine, introduction to juicing, adding in any helpful supplements as suggestions, energy work, restoring of the spirit, and intuitive works to do my best to get the client balanced. This is *devotion* work that doctors either are not trained for at all, or simply do not have the time for. Often they must stay in the confines of a codified system of diagnosing disease and have perhaps ten minutes per patient.

For my Guidance sessions, I initially require an hour to gather information: hear their story, ask about digestion, elimination, sleep, sex drive, diet in part, and more.

Shamans were once respected as the first community Medicine People. Of course, many Shamans were Elders, over 50 years of age, because they had walked a road.

In my case, I have owned businesses, raised a child on my own, had biological family issues, relocated thousands of miles from home, faced incredible diagnoses, endured police issues, racial issues, discrimination issues and had extensive communication trainings and learning from life. I am cross-cultural and have had an extensive professional background, working in law for nearly eighteen years in San Jose, California and Santa Cruz. I have herbal, Ayurvedic, intuitive, massage, and a culmination of lifetime experiences and developments that also mesh well with my dharma (natural born tendencies) as a Cancer in astrological terms. And, I have learned to communicate, even with Rohini in my chart.

As Shamans, we often perform Guidance in teaching as I did through Community Education and Whole Foods Cooperative stores, and other places. Bringing more natural ways to the community.

My life experiences have brought me to offer Readings, Wellness Consultations, Spiritual Guidance and Canine Assistance, from feeding, health, and guidance.

Eventually, we get comfortable in our own skin and turn to helping others to be comfortable in theirs too. Sometimes that means breaking down reality and truth in a way for the client to comprehend the changes to make in their life and for their health or a family member, and creating a plan for now; possibly goals for later.

Many years ago, I read the works of James Redfield, in his *Celestine Prophecy*[1] series which greatly enhanced my understandings in my practice and personal life about synchronicities. It is additionally where I began using the term "control drama."

I have learned to pay attention to spirit: the way messages, synchronicities come about and to pay attention to energy. I have been on this path as an advanced practitioner now for many decades and so sensing and my being this way is quite natural. I can sense using my inner compass well now.

That inner compass or what I often refer to as one's "inner GPS" is how many times I had just known something; been somehow shown the way, to each next layer of knowledge. Many refer to this as intuition.

This is how you notice and are led to the next synchronous event. And, in part, how you stay out of control drama.

---

[1] Redfield, James. *The Celestine Prophecy: An Adventure.* Bantam Publishing. 1985.

My Ancestors and Spirit Guides have been many and have been very active in my works. The Shaman is a storyteller and I have so many stories to share that I hope to over time. Many times in my weakness, my Ancestors have shown up and done my work for me, knowing how to protect me, carry me, and give me direct messages. I never expect from them, they pleasantly surprise me with gifts.

I often share with clients that when I do readings with cards based on human archetypes, I only utilize the Field (or the higher, intuitive self) that they are not accessing at this time. This is a way to get readings which involve decisions.

At about four years old, I learned to leave my body and travel through the walls of my bedroom. I remember seeing many sights and I remember my totem animal coming for these trips each time. One, two or three wolves showed up on the left side of my bed near the wall.

Part of what preceded my family member working with me was that my maternal grandmother lost her first born son, Dennis and the hurt was palpable, of course. It was the year I was born. She was a student of Dr. Ian Stevenson, a psychiatrist who focused on reincarnation research, and also reading Zecharia Sitchin's work[2]. She began working with me to open my heartmind. I began with billet readings, Ouija board, and other tools. I did very well and she additionally

_____

[2] Sitchin, Zecharia. http://www.sitchin.com/

took me to see a lady in San Francisco, who was Priestess. That same woman had warts on my left hand removed in ten days energetically.

Around the time I was eight, I was living in San Jose, California. I was the caretaker for our two chow chow dogs named Red and Peewee. I loved them so much. They were my companions.

I also spent many hours with the monkeys, large birds and the Manx cats we lived with. I would stay outside on the patio and be with the passion flowers that grew in the vine along the fence, just observing them, being with them.

One day a famous astrologer and psychic came to get one of the puppies that were from the chow chow litter of Red and Peewee who I had named Star. The lady wanted to know more about me because she had fully intended to name this little pup, this sweet black female puppy, Star.

In an attempt to please my grandmother, I did my best to do what she asked in terms of developing my 'sight.' Beginning at about age eight with billet readings, she would draw an image, a letter or a word and hold it silently behind her back, daily developing my insight and ability to use my young spirit, fresh from the rainbow bridge of the spirit world to connect with her son Dennis, somehow. Some days we would use the Ouija board, which was not my favorite. I did not like the entities that would show up sometimes.

Often, people would invite me to go see or meet a Shaman, Psychic, Reader or such, and I have been disappointed at times. I like to receive readings and guidance, but learned to primarily read for myself. I have gone to scores of folks out of interest or for fun over the many years who offer similar services as myself, but the majority of the time, I leave disappointed. For all their mystical accoutrements, pictures, and talk, my intuition can clearly pick up on the lack of abilities they claim.

Ancestors are energy. They are now in, what I call, the "Field." Some have more audible presence and some have been capable of showing images in the far/third eye of what formerly their matter presented like.

In order to perceive the Field, it is important to vibrate high and focus on how you live, what you eat, righteous living, all is a part of it. We use our glandular system: pineal, pituitary, thyroid, all are part of how we sense and feel. Not everybody feels or eats the same way. For me, I have found that my personal vibration is not as strong eating flesh foods, dairy products and chemicals that are in a lot of our foods today. I have felt a direct correlation to my sensing, intuition and my diet. Vibration is everything.

Clean food sources and staying away from the heavy emotional vibe in the factory-farmed animals living their lives in captivity, crowded and emotionally pained is a first step.

The sentient beings are forced to live under some very harmful and stressful conditions which cause those emotions that flow through the blood to enter the being and thus, the meat.

Of all the tools, if asked which was the most largely instrumental and helpful, I would have to say meditation. It has saved my life.

Shamans use a trance-like state of mind that is entered through meditation. Nothing fancy, but occasionally a sacramental or ceremonial dose of a plant, cannabis, has created pathways for those centers to be opened and alive and sensing in this life; particularly for people who were not brought up as babies in this tradition. The plant world has much to share and they lend incredible pathways and experiences, as do the trees. I learned a lot from trees, just sitting with my back or front with a tree and listening; downloading.

So, you can glean from what I share here that Medicine people are not doctors. Many of us really simply either are not interested or do not have the time to learn all the Latin names for each bone, tendon, ligament, coded disease. We see the disease as a lack of ease. We heal from the Root, applying what I have shared, hearing the story and facilitating moving the energy. Once you experience it, you will understand. I have watched many of my clients leave the shop where I rent space claiming it "was a miracle."

I have used song with my young children clients to help move energy and to move hurts. And, often the song just comes to me; the right song to sing, hum, or chant. The children seem to enjoy it too.

I have briefly studied Jyotish (Vedic astrology), as I use these teachings often as tools in my medicine bag. I look for omens, nature, the living world, vibrations. I am the patient observer during the course of listening with the client.

After all, we live in an energy soup! It is what I sense around us, all the time. I feel energies, sense omens, like noticing birds, animals crossing my path and I theirs. Noticing directions they fly, what side of my path they are on when I sight them. And, much more. I notice spiders that come my way (Anancy) and I notice and hear several inner guidance voices. When clients are on the table in session, I feel and sense the energies moving in their bodies.

All of this is our innate gift of life. Life is beautiful, and to be celebrated while we are here. That is why the ankh is shaped like a key, the key of life. Both a womb and a phallic symbol incorporated into one symbol, evidencing the partnership of male and female. We are a people who contain many memories; we walk *with* the Ancestors.

The first time I heard the Ancestors, I heard them so loud and clear. I was in the middle of a drum and dance circle, in Los Gatos at the *Los Gatos Coffee Roasting Company*, the owner had given a large group of us a place to play and dance and relax. I will never forget the powerful female voices that sang into my ears and, for all intents and purposes, time stopped and I entered the dreamtime.

I have entered the dreamtime more deeply over the many years that have passed since that day in the early 1990s, certainly as I deepen into the heartbeat of life. I took one of the courses from *HeartMath*[3] located in Boulder Creek, California, and really loved their concept of "entrainment" of the heart. Our heart energies are electric! Our heart beat is more powerful than even our brain electrical signals; the EKG is larger than the EEG. When we align ourselves with another in close proximity or even remotely, there is evidence in bilocational healing; our sending that heartbeat energy to another recipient.

Most people are only familiar with work in the present moment of time, yet in Gregg Braden's book, *The Divine Matrix*[4], he talks about bilocation. There are many examples which, despite our views of physics today, prove that something can be in one place and somewhere else

---

[3] *HeartMath*. http://www.heartmath.com/
[4] Braden, Gregg. *The Divine Matrix*. New York: Hay House, Inc. 2007.

simultaneously. Proven by mystics, yogis and medicine people from the 16th and 17th centuries and today, people, too, have bilocated. This also is how remote viewing, remote sensing, and remote healing works – directing intent through consciousness to a precise location.

Padre Pio and Maria de Agreda are referenced, but also empirical proof of bilocation and healing demonstrate the efficacy of healing with our energy even from far distances, apart from one another, by those with focused intent and energy.

What we can do with this great loving ability! I often do distance or remote work with great results, although many are unfamiliar with this type of work. *How does that work?* they wonder. And I briefly explain bilocation, as well as with readings where I intuit.

I have had many Facebook connections whom I have never met in person, as many of us do today, and I have awoken from a dream or had a feeling about them and sent them a message. In these instances, I have had the information confirmed, and a reply: "How on earth did you know this?" they question. "Wow, I have no idea how you do this!" they exclaim with awe.

I have had messages from a spirit, including about my son's grandfather. I heard that he may pass in a month from a heart issue and I called my family to let them know, of course, feeling awkward about relating that message but to do my best to deliver it as delicately as possible. This did come to pass and is why some people do fear this gift at times.

The Field has shown me that essentially we are one, separated by the simpleton habit of sensing separation. If you want to test this, send some energy out and watch how it comes back.

I believe that formerly, we relied on a good amount of telepathic communication. However, the uses of cell phones, and the removal of the drum, and turning to the internet have caused us to resort to other ways to experience communication and language. Our grammatical structural language "forms" have actually caused abilities to become receded and reduced our abilities to connect with a larger source of information and guidance. In the Field, you will find all.

When I enter the meditative state which I have learned to enter so frequently over decades now, I can sense things often unnoticed by many. There, I find colors and symbols. There, I hear them. I have often heard names of clients' relatives in this relaxed way, and saw and heard messages like one from a client of mine named Deb regarding an immediate issue with her breasts. I have worked with clients in the ICU and regained their strengths utilizing energy work, including Deb's son.

When people in a small city trust you, and that trust takes a bit longer for sure, they send their entire families to see you. Even if you are the foreigner that arrived from California and you possibly look or talk differently than they do.

One of my clients who is now residing in New Mexico is a lovely man who had a history of kidney issues, trouble walking and used a cane. He was single for quite a while. He had heard about my work and, for the summers, came to Minnesota where he was raised and had family and a daughter, and then left for the winters. He was very thankful and expressed that he no longer needed his cane after one treatment of energy work and massage. We also then did a Wellness Consultation and improved his diet, finding things he was willing to eat. He called me so very thankful. Being a veteran, he had visited Mayo Clinic and they were really surprised that his kidney issues were vastly improved.

One of the last times I saw him while he was up here, I had a strong intuition of a woman entering his life and related with him about what I saw. He was in a place where he really wanted that to happen. It was a period of months later that he asked me for a distance reading and then months after that he sent me a text with a picture of his new mate and their companion (dog).

I have assisted elder men with prostate issues, reversed diabetes, and one of my all-time favorites is helping clients find balance when Ancestors were trying to reach them.

When I go to bed to sleep, I often "vision" which is different than dreaming. It has become a habit now. Some of my sleep time is usually filled with travel, meeting others, and I hear that I am supposed to write and teach in many places in the world.

If you can believe that we all have potential to develop these abilities, it would be absolutely wonderful if we could put our focus on developing them, increasing them, and looking for ways to increase and develop not only our understandings, but the way we communicate, how we do it, how we communicate in an observation-based way, not a judgment way.

Healing the
MindBody

Moving Depression

Lisa[5] caught up with me while she sat in the hair chair at our local day spa.

One of the ladies there said to me, "Shaman, your client wants to speak with you. She's sitting in my hair chair and she just saw you."

I finished up resetting my table and came out promptly. Lisa asked if she could get in today and I was able to fit her in that afternoon.

When she came into my treatment room, she exclaimed, "Oh, it smells so good in here! It feels so good!"

I gave her a moment to get herself ready for our session before I came back to knocked on her door. I checked her bolster under her knees, put a warmed breast cover on her, a warmed heart pillow, brushed her hair back from around her face tenderly with my hand, as to increase safety, warmth and connection. This all encourages the opening of the Field.

I then placed the warmed eye pillow over a tissue on her eyes. Next, I sat in my usual position on my stool behind her head at the front of the table, rubbing her hair and temples.

---

[5] *Some names have been changed to protect client privacy*

There was in my far eye an image of two tall wheat stalks. I had no idea what that meant, but knowing from past experience that it would make sense later , I continued, having a few more images. I continued to work around her body and she spoke as I got to her legs asking if I noticed a lot of stress in her body.

"A bit, yes," I replied. *But what about the wheat stalks?* I wondered, silently to myself.

It was a quiet environment – the two of us in that private room, yoga type music playing – and it remained silent for what felt like five minutes and then she spoke up saying:

"My childhood memories that remind me of happy times are playing in the wheat fields."

She had shared earlier that she felt she lost so much, and shared just what she felt she lost and was to rebuild. She had also informed me that she felt as though she lost herself by gaining weight, feeling so tired all the time, that she no longer really liked her job so much and more.

It was when I got to the stomach that she brought up the wheat fields. The stomach is an important piece to this work. It is important to use a clockwise motion when you work with belly energy.

At the end of our session, I worked hard removing stagnant grief from her left ribcage. Lisa winced a bit as I know that area is so very sensitive. I was never taught in any school or book about this, but learned that in protecting the heart, the ribcage area can get very congested in self-protection, so I check it with my clients, just like I balance their thyroid reflex point on the big toe.

Earlier, I had a moment feeling the Egyptian Goddess, Het Heru – "the Womb of Origin" – and feeling some things integrate into my body and my heartmind. Earlier I would have called this a "download" because, in part, it was.

When Lisa came back for a wellness consultation later in the evening as she wanted to do this as soon as possible. We worked through some important things and she is now excited to begin a new journey.

DEPRESSION AND INFERTILITY

A friend referred Ann to me and she booked both a table treatment and a wellness consultation hour. Ann had never worked with a Shaman before but was very open to the new experience. She had resided in a variety of places throughout her life and had the insight only developed by adapting to learning new environments and the opportunities afforded working in a networking and corporate arena.

We were scheduled by telephone through a family member for our time and when I did link up with her with my headset on, ready with note paper and pens, cards and such, she asked if she could call back in five minutes because she was trying to wrap something up. I knew very little about her but I did know that she wanted a baby. That 'want' was bringing on some depression.

She had heard of the talk of my upcoming book regarding the importance of caring for our wombs. The womb is vital. It carries so much information and we need to pay more attention to our organs and to our Yonis.

I waited and she called back but I could not hear her. I, of course, paid attention to these omens (her being busy and then our call becoming disconnected.) not unlike I would pay attention to any particular birds in the Field, clouds, storms, winds from which direction, and more. These omens are a part of the "Medicine."

I wrote that on the top of the page. Maybe it was meaningful, maybe it wasn't. Once we were able to connect on our phone call, I asked her a few basic questions and jotted down some notes, such as her "Moon" time, blood type, current diet, sleep, any diagnosis and so forth. During the first session, a little bit of time is required in gathering this information and parts of her story arrive in this "gathering." It is my basket.

I learned of Ann feeling cold a lot, depression happening despite never receiving prevention guidance, a diagnosis nor drugs administered for it as well as some other issues including not being able to conceive a child.

I informed her that there are several considerations in a case such as this. Spiritual, physical, physiology, emotional, MindBody components are all areas that I peruse in order to ascertain the best path.

We talked for a little while longer and, much later in the conversation, in order to cover much ground, I splayed out six cards to search her Field. The cards revealed to me that she searched for a new occupation and she anticipated many trips.

"Have you felt disconnected and busy?" I asked her.

"Yes!" she replied, clearly impressed with my observation. "I am busy and disconnected and I don't want to have this type of life any longer!"

I read another card and it indicated she was a viable candidate for a Family Traditions based business and I indicated two possibilities, both of which she really liked. They bridged the gap further in terms of her feeling a bit isolated lately and if a baby was coming, they allowed more time at home and while requiring little or no trips.

A Shaman facilitates for the whole person. We address all important areas – spiritual, MindBody, emotional – by also bridging with our experiences in the world and outside of this world.

As the phone call continued, we went over some dietary changes and some ideas she would like to implement into her diet as well as incorporating some Kemetic (Egyptian) Yoga which is perfect for getting more blood flow to the Yoni.

This is what I do. We had a very power packed session for which she was glad to pay and I heard back that she was thankful, feeling the services I offered were very valuable.

Ann had a doctor, a husband, a few close friends, a homeopath and an acupuncturist but she needed a Shaman!

Sessions such as this are the reason why I love what I do. I've put my heart into investing into these works for myself and I can gift tremendous insight into reversing any disease and gaining strengths in the life. Taking a leap of faith and finding the Root is beneficial for our entire being.

A woman, Felicia, called me one morning asking about an appointment. She said that one of her closest friends had recommended me and she had waited a year before contacting me. She was anxious to make an appointment and inquired whether I had anything available soon.

"How about today?" I offered.

I heard a bit of anger in her voice as I asked the usual initial questions.

"Do you have any allergies or health conditions I need to be aware of for energy and bodywork?"

"I have a nut allergy," she indicated. I could feel a bit more of that jaw tension as she and I found a time on the calendar. I agreed to see her later in the day.

When Felicia arrived, I saw a beautiful woman near to my age with a nice glow. She seemed quite happy and had open, receptive eyes. I showed her around to the treatment room and I went to wash up.

Immediately after placing a warmed eye pillow, I began to see a shade of green, and recognized it as the flavor and shade I normally "feel" when sensing Heart chakra issues.

I had never met her before our session, and we did not share anything but her health and a quick check in as to any potential to allergies before starting. Since she was a completely new client, I had perused her health history form that she completed prior to our session.

As we began the hour, Felicia was quiet, as was I. We were surrounded by the gentle glow of candle light and yoga type music filled the room. The room lights were dimmed down low to help with the sense of peace and relaxation.

I easily sensed that her right foot was noticeably energetically colder than any other part of her. Her right calf was also cooler and less "present" energetically.

The right side is often considered the Sun side and typically house male energy or work while the left is the Moon side, usually Female. While this may not always be the case, years of work have given me the experience to decipher this easily when working with each individual client.

The bodywork was completed and she had seen my sign about offering readings. She asked for a bottle of the transdermal Iodine I retail for $15 as her friend had told her about my thyroid knowledge and workshops. Age, geography and her moods, she knew that she had read about Iodine and it would be a good investment.

Felicia asked for a half hour reading session and, as she left the room, I tidied up to prepare the room to sit down and use the cards and intuition.

As we readied for the reading session, the woman related to me that I had provided her the best massage and bodywork she had ever received I was humbly thankful for the compliment!

I listened intently as she related her story and said that she wasn't sure if she wanted to let go of her current relationship. She had put years into it.

After she finished asking her question, I laid two jump cards on the table: the Nine of Pentacles which told me money was a factor. She indicated loud and clear that that was absolutely true and then, as she continued in her story, I laid the Hermit card. She needed some solo time. She longed for it. And, again, she confirmed that she did.

I splayed the deck and asked her to pick three cards and face them towards her. She selected the High Priestess, the Queen of Wands (reversed) and the King of Pentacles. I explained each card's meaning: the Pentacles relates to mind and money while the Wands to relationships.

Felicia was an Aries sign and this Reading had everything to do with her being the one to make the decision, while he held the finances and the money. Her power was an issue here.

We went into more detail which she excitedly confirmed and was thankful she had chosen to do the reading. Commenting that the experience was very satisfying, she felt these things to be true and I, again, related it was from her Higher Self. I am only the conduit, the tool.

Felicia was a talented woman and we both agreed that fear can have you in its grip. That we both want for a goal and that former poverty states and the state of the world combined with our being in our fifties has us both less inclined to risk and jump out and leave behind what we do have, what we have built.

TREATING LUPUS

I was contact through a friend regarding her long time friend, Ashleigh, who was diagnosed nearly 25 years ago with Lupus.

"There is so much going on in my life at this time," my friend expressed to me. "My dear friend is not well and is suffering. Can you help her? I can't think of anyone better to help her besides you. I trust you!"

"Of course!" I told her. "I would be honored."

I called Ashleigh and we began meeting for weekly wellness consultations by phone. We were both from California and had similar job histories in Executive Administration, so this gave me an inkling of the type of work she was doing at the time. I worked as a Senior Paralegal in Family law for nearly eighteen years, which was very similar to her work.

She related she was in her early 20s when she was diagnosed with Lupus. Of course, I wanted to hear what was manifesting at this time and I listened carefully for the Root causes. When somebody gains a comfort with you, when they trust you, you begin to hear it. Not everybody trusts easily in the first meeting, and just like many diagnosed diseases, not every issue which has been present can be worked through in a short time.

So to begin, I listened for the MindBody causative, or what I refer to as the Root. From there, I listened and familiarized myself with her manifesting symptoms, heard her history that preceded the onset of the disease, and inquired about her true dietary intake, other health conditions or allergies. As I often do, I asked about energy levels, sleep, water intake, exercise, and sexual drive. With this information, I can get a good sense through using my Intuition of the basis for what is happening.

In these cases, I find it helpful to use my cards to access the Higher Field which often, those who are focused on healing or in the midst of a healing crisis as this client was, may not be able to access on their own.

I seek to strengthen. I seek to form a union with her true self (Sat Nam), her vibration. I seek the Goddess self, Higher Self, to restore her back to her homeostasis.

Ashleigh and I had many phone sessions and I followed up with her often. We worked together one weekend and she informed me that she had been juicing and healing well. We talked about some future endeavors in order to remain future focused.

It is my belief that many clients with Myasthenia Gravis, Crohn's Disease, diabetes, low energy, hair loss, Hemochromatosis, thyroid issues, cancers of all types, metabolic issues, Lyme's Disease, Attention Deficit Disorder, Spirit/Entity possession, and more need a combination of nutritional balance, energetic balance, and often need vocational balance. Massage is also an excellent tool to move energy and encourage healing.

In my line of work, I seek to restore balance and homeostasis such that the client can remove most or all of the medications and drugs dispensed by doctors and I am always delighted when I find Western Allopathic Doctors who choose to partner with Medicine People.

Intuitive healers such as myself heal by making food our medicine, incorporating super foods, utilizing energy work, partnering with our spiritual allies (Ancestor work), focusing on our life purpose and encouraging kindred healing.

Many of my clients and myself have experienced Western medical doctors who tell us that these diseases will be with us for the rest of our lives. It has been thirty years, and I have personally walked myself and many others through the river of life in terms of healing, restoring self and balance.

Guidance is important. It is part of the medicine. We get into patterns, some are self-defeating for sundry reasons, others are food-related, and still others are addictive. I have also worked with people housing spirit walk-ins. This comes often from abusing substances and having issues that were not addressed in healing their field.

When I spoke with Ashleigh by phone during one of our last sessions, I wondered about the skin issues associated with Lupus. I began to ask questions about her past. She was forthcoming and she entered the flow as she responded. I felt the stream of energy move as she related the history of her past. Her mother, herself, how she interpreted her childhood, and what she wished she may have had.

She shared about her gallbladder and I related about gallbladder energy and its connection with liver and repressed anger. We spoke in detail about some of the anger she formerly carried and perhaps to some extent still carries today. We also conversed about expectations, particularly of those closest to us.

Lupus had come during a time in her life when she was experiencing some very negative situations in her life. The doctor had diagnosed this disease when those symptoms were present and then and until this day, she had been placed upon medications that likely were equally harmful to the disease, in my opinion.

Lupus also joined Ashleigh with her mother again, her friend again, and joined the friend that referred her to me, thus joining the three of us. All of us wanting to, perhaps, move closer to one another at a point in time.

She is highly likely to be able to do this work, change the diet, move the MindBody energy and likely will be able to remove the medications. I look forward to her journey, as we have much work still to do to unravel the effects of the long term medication use and to equip her for the future with tools that she needs and wants.

We get past the healing crisis now, into detoxification, into steady new patterns, adding minerals, adding other components and the body will take over.

Many years ago, having read so many books during a few decades of my life, I had the privilege of reading Dr. John Sarno's book *The Divided Mind*[6]. He gave examples as I am doing here where he works with clients with tremendous pain and how as professor and practicing physician he alleviates this pain nearly 100% through MindBody medicine.

Dr. Sarno calls these syndromes, tenso myositis syndromes or "TMS." They are essentially, he says, "oxygen deprivations."

Shamans, the last of the real, true Shamans, hear, listen, feel, move with the clients, know their medicine well, and they are proven, decades of healing, facilitating health and healing, using food as medicine, moving energy, ancestor works, and plenty of decades of guiding in many capacities. There are not many of us left any more.

FEELING THE GUIDES

Maybe you call them "Spirit Guides." Some may refer to them as "Ancestors." But this share happened one

[6] Sarno, James E., M.D. *The Divided Mind: The Epidemic of Mindbody Disorders*. Regan Books. 2006.

morning with my client, Judy, and it has happened many times before with clients on my side of the table.

Judy had been a client of mine for years, and this specific morning she had a massage and energy work session. I began seeing her husband for treatments a few years before she had come in. Her husband convinced her and she has since become my primary client out of the two of them.

Judy is a Finn, in her late 60s and I may have assumed she was a bit slower to accept newer, less conservative ideas.

Yet she and I are close and often talk about many things, and although she is not the most demonstrative person, she is warm in her own way. This was a little more of that learning that I have done from relocating to Minnesota, as the area has a large amount of Northern Scandinavian people whose culture tends to be less expressive.

I believe that I am perhaps an energy worker and massage therapist for her as well as somebody who listens and cares. That MindBody piece is one reason why many clients will return as being heard in today's world is vital. It is actually crucial.

Judy and I spoke many times about a family situation that was causing her some stress.

When she came in one day, I spent some extra time with her, about 25 minutes, as I knew that as a longtime client she was going through some things. I also had the personal time on my calendar in order to be able to gift quality listening time. She wanted some suggestions and I offered them, informing her that I truly felt that the manifestations were more MindBody than anything.

I saw that she looked a little bit more weary than her normal self that day. She was a casual but healthful vibrant older woman who enjoyed gardening and we would often share about her dog as well. During this session, she shared that she had some little "bursts of headaches" recently. She saw her optometrist who gave her a prescription for eye drops which she said took away her dry eye.

I asked her to please join us in our next thyroid workshop, letting her know that it would benefit both her and her husband.

I was sure to mention that we live in a large goiter belt and that the states surrounding the Great Lakes region have the highest incidents of thyroid problems; nearly 60 to 80% of the population according to a few doctors of whom I cite in my workshops.

Judy was on the table and face up, which is how I started this particular treatment and most of my treatments. She was relaxing and quiet as we did our talking before our session. The room was entirely quiet. As I worked on her right arm, I felt an energy and I also felt an obstruction which was leading to her heart center.

I then took off her warm eye pillow and she looked up at me saying, "Your hands were both on my head and face and yet I felt a hand grasp my hand and hold on and not let go for a few moments."

It is important to note that Judy is somebody who is very mentally stable and conservative.

She went on to say, "That was really weird!" In her disbelief, she repeated again, "I know for a fact a hand was holding onto my hand and I know it wasn't you!"

"It was your right hand," I told her.

She replied, "Yes. You know. How do you know?"

I kept quiet as I finished out our session and as she lay face down in the face cradle, I could tell she had some goosebumps on her skin. I turned the heater up a bit just to comfort her.

I could feel that she was beginning to sense what I sense. She was beginning to understand that they are always with us.

Dear reader, how about you? I wonder how many of you reading this have experienced anything like this. Have you had a hand to hold on to? Felt somebody doing energy work where you actually felt the hand, or the person, or their breath?

Myself, this has happened many times, including when I was about to have a surgery and was still working to keep our boat afloat with my son and I and after returning to my business. I had clients tell me that they felt the other person. I have actually seen the other Ancestors working on them. I know they helped me out before.

One client saw a very frail, elder African woman working on their feet while I worked on their top half of her body.

This is so often what it is like on my side of the table.

SUICIDE OR ACCIDENT?

His email showed up in my inbox asking for a reading. I apologized that I had not seen his message from February in my "other" folder. He wanted to schedule right away and did for himself and his daughter, who was a young adult.

His name was Aaron and we met by phone, along with his daughter, Melanie. The phone call was for a basic ten minute reading.

Melanie was first and she asked about her partner, a woman. I got a card that showed something had happened and she knew that the relationship was not a good choice in the long run. We expounded further and then she asked another question, all within the 10 minutes. During our call, she was jubilant and I related that something specific that had happened that day and elaborated about it.

"How did you know?" she questioned.

I said, "It's all in your Field!"

Next I spoke with her father. Aaron asked about his vocation expressing that he was not happy with what he was doing. The cards showed legal work and specifically family law. I shared briefly that I had a nearly eighteen year career in various capacities in family law and he said he wasn't sure because he thought, maybe he was too old. I saw, "Nah. You're just right!"

Our time was up, and Aaron said, "I do have a burning question, please."

"Sure!" I encouraged. "I have a few moments."

He paused for a moment, clearly composing himself before asking such a weighted question.

"My former partner," he mumbled. "Was it a suicide or an accident?"

Focusing very intently, I drew three cards.

"I see water," I said, almost instinctively. "She died in water."

"Oh, my God!" Aaron exclaimed, breathlessly. "She did! She drowned in a few inches of water!"

I continued. "There was foul play. I am uncertain as how to answer your question."

Aaron seemed very content with my response and he and his daughter both indicated that they would be back, and that they would be telling their friends.

Even if I won the lottery tomorrow and never needed to work, these are the moments that remind me that I would still teach and do wellness and readings. I wouldn't need the money. And that is when you know you are doing what you love.

WHOLE PERSON SHAMANIC WORKS

When Joann scheduled her online wellness consult, she indicated the following: stomach issues, elimination issues migraines, lack of energy, waking unrested, weight issues, food intolerances, and excess skin on the hands and feet. Considering the long list of unbalances, I gathered information for some time, considerably longer than usual, given that my first responsibility is "to do no harm."

The Hippocratic Oath is what doctors and all practitioners are supposed to deliver – health, prevention, and no harm.

I listened to her MindBody story and intuitively saw a few things. I then drew a few cards, accessing her field. She resided in the United Kingdom yet, while we shared by email on a social media, I brought up pictures of her to remotely tap into her Field.

I could see how the blockage manifested through self-protection, fear, grief, and even anger. When a young person feels helpless and they have nowhere to escape the madness of the adults around them, they internalize. In her case, putting on "Pounds of Pain" which is done for insulating, protection, and hoping to cause rejection of unwanted energy.

Joann had not entirely let go of the way her mind and body had created this protection but she was on the river of self-love which I honored and loved and tended to in her "soil."

People who have been overeating often create the symbiotic host opportunity for candida and parasites, and I would also say that most people today struggle with this to some degree due to our society's heavy sugar intake.

People come to me with all manner of "heat" psoriasis, eczema, and dandruff and we talk about reduction of candida. To reverse the candida process too fast is to create a "die off" that is not fun. It tends to leave many feeling ill and struggling with flu-like symptoms.

That level of detoxing is too fast for most people as they feel miserable and then likely sense that the process is not working, considering they feel equally miserable or worse. For this reason, I always recommend my clients gradually decrease the levels of parasites and candida in the body using probiotics and changing most of their diet. I sense where they are and guide them through the process so they can feel good in their own body.

It was my 'art' to build her, to strengthen her and to foster some good habits so that she could increase – through her life and her health – and promote herself as the true Goddess she was.

She received her guidance from me, from my highest sense of goodwill and, as I always do, I still keep her in my thoughts, as I do all who have come to me.

I gave Joann a list of a few things to purchase from a natural foods store as well as an idea on some things to not eat during this time (or ever) and some lifestyle changes in terms of sleep and habits.

Even as our two hour session came to a close, I additionally gave her a reading she desired about finding a potential mate in her life, providing her with the whole person Shamanic works of which I offer.

FINDING HUMAN POTENTIAL

Jessica called the Day Spa seeking a massage and the receptionist booked her with me. I wasn't sure I really wanted to go in again that day. I was a little tired from a long week with many uphills and downhills and plenty of repairs and highs and lows.

I had seen a client at 8:00 that morning and handled a bunch of issues on my house but I decided to shower and go in. Before leaving the house, I made myself a large superfood jar of juice as a pick-me-up: a mason jar of lemonade juicing two lemons and shook with filtered water and some coconut palm sugar. I called Jessica and told her I could come in. I would go and give my best! She said she really needed it and wanted some deep tissue on her shoulders, neck and back.

When she arrived at the Day Spa, she recalled, "Oh, I know you! I remember your son."

She completed the health history form which is required of all first time clients. After which I escorted her to the treatment room and related that she could start face up. She indicated she only wanted half of her body done.

"Okay," I replied. "But I generally prefer to balance the whole body and because you have tension on your shoulders, I work the reflexology points on your feet, and particularly your toes, to release some of this. Otherwise, the one half of the body is unbalanced."

"Well, okay," she said, sheepishly. Then she jokingly added, "But I haven't shaved my legs!"

"No problem! In the cold we have been having, below zero many mornings, I haven't either! The hair keeps us warmer!" I quipped.

After a moment of shared laughter, Jessica asked more seriously, "that part on the medical history form about Shamanic works? I don't know what that is."

"Do you know what a medicine person is?"

She responded, "Yes, I work with one."

"Well," I continued, "this is nearly the same."

"The medicine man I work with, he tells me stuff about myself. How does he know this?"

I went on to share for a few minutes longer about what medicine people generally are.

I then left while she undressed and readied herself for our session. I came back with a gentle knock on the treatment room door and we began.

As I worked with her body, mind, and spirit, I noticed several things. First, that she kept her hands tightly close to her body. I would gently come up under her hands and move them a bit of distance from her sides both for my ability to work with her and also to encourage her to feel comfortable. It is not that unusual for a first time client to do this.

Her body was very tightly wound and controlled, packaged. More than I had seen before, frankly. Jessica was a Finlander. There are many in Minnesota from Finland and the community can be very conservative and tightly controlled.

I noticed several things in our session, and I saw several images working on her including an ankh. Why of all things with this woman?

My Guides began to say, *she will listen with you and she has a major shift that will lead her to be one of the allies of our time.*

I could have doubted for sundry reasons, but I have an excellent memory of my own personal journey and I have learned to trust the Ancestors in a very special way. I do not disrespect nor doubt the Ancestors when I hear it. I must listen.

At the end of our session, she came out, kind of poker faced, but I saw the shift.

"I really liked that," she said. "I am tense, huh?"

"You are tight and highly controlled."

"I know. I am teaching this and yet it is something I must work on too."

I related that we go into jobs where we ourselves often need balance. For the time I worked in family law, for different reasons, it balanced me and I learned from it – communication, articulation.

Jessica was on several medications and I mentioned that I also could tell she had some easy to address issues in reference to her health. Fixing her adrenals, thyroid and releasing some of her tensions with regular sessions would really help her.

I decided to relay what I had heard from the Ancestors, telling her that she will be offered a major life switch and I explained what that might look like. It appeared as a possibility to change directions geographically and in her work, somewhat to be open to it and not to immediately reject it, even though it took her a distance from her family for a time.

With this, she began to open up. "I am not open to hugs. I do not communicate much. I stay very closed. You are right."

I stayed later with her because, you see, this is the medicine. It is planting seeds. Every single day I plant the seeds of medicine and you do and can too!

With our families, our neighbors, people we meet, our children, their partners, people we coach, people we work with.

When Jessica left, she said she would check into my teaching at the Reservation to the nurses, clinicians, social workers, and doctors and agreed to take my card to the Medicine Man she worked with.

She recognized that the Medicine Man and I were similar in many ways. We have an inner knowing and a well-developed tool of guidance. She was amazed that we both told her very similar things that just anybody could not possibly have known and that they were both very similar.

I am glad I decided to go in to that session. It meant I gave up my gym time but I gained in so many more ways. Out of many comes one heart!

HANDCUFFS?

Laurie was a first time client. She came in at the end of the day. She had called the day spa and was seeking body work and massage.

She didn't say much, except that she wanted some deep tissue in a few places. I gathered that she was in her forties. After she completed the paperwork, I escorted her to my treatment room. I showed her the room and asked her to start by lying on her back.

She was really happy to get on the table and start feeling better. I kidded that I am a "hair wrecker" and that if any of that mattered, to please let me know. "Otherwise," I informed her, "I make the assumption that you are here to relax and I get into your scalp and soothe those nerve-endings."

I facilitated a journey by asking her to breathe deeply into her belly and relax her mind, releasing any tensions and to breathe in new joy, balance, while breathing out anything that no longer served her. She then went quiet.

In our warm room, where it was so cold outside, the candle burned and beautiful music played through a CD, the table warmed, and the room quiet, I began my work.

* * *

I helped her unleash her worries, sending them to the outreaches of the Universe and causing them to exit our space.

I reached under her back as I was seated on a stool at the head of the table, her warmed eye pillow over her eyes and the room darkened just enough to fully relax. And I felt, but I also saw, several images.

I worked further down her arms, felt the tensions release, down to her legs, using my spearmint eucalyptus lotion. Then, I saw a blue diamond heart on a gentle necklace. The blue was crystal clear.

Later, I saw the handcuffs? What did this mean? I let it go.

But I got the feeling she was no longer in control and the blue signified it was related with males in her life. She had the classic mother wound on her left shoulder top that I've become used to identifying.

At the end of our session, I asked about the images and as is often the case, Laurie was confused.

"You saw?" she questioned, a quizzical look on her face.

"Yes," I responded, in a matter of fact way. "I saw a pair of handcuffs. What are the struggles with males?"

She said, "My two sons. They no longer speak with me. They won't."

Inside, I thought, *you certainly are not the only one!* There are far too many that I see, struggling in this same area.

She continued, "And I divorced a real jerk!" That explained the blue diamond necklace in a heart shape. She explained further and we both laughed, kindredly. I reminded her to be thankful for this day as life changes day by day and that she could carry the glow of this session with her.

I also identified several glaring thyroid issues for which the traditional doctors placed her on mood stabilizers and anti-depressants. These are not medicine. These are drugs. Our plants, they are medicine. What we make with our love, is medicine.

I may not always look forward to my hours of giving massage many days a week, but I always look forward to the people, to the love, to what I learn, massage, medicine woman, people by phone, through social media, and, for this, I am blessed!

SENSING A FORMER PARTNER

Kara's partner had passed several days prior to our meeting, and she spoke of her, having been her caregiver. She said that the lawyers were taking care of her partner's estate now. That things were locked off from her.

I told Kara that I sensed her former partner was a woman also that she is a lesbian/bi-sexual woman and that there was somebody talking of being out on a "branch." During our meeting, I was shown a few more things.

You see, when you learn to sense the Field, you sense from Far/Third Eye. It's greatly enhanced when you are relaxed, on a plant-based diet, and when you are seasoned with frequently entering into a relaxed, meditative state. As one who has been working with clients for many decades, I have learned to sense it and speak with it.

I often sense the departed. It has been over four decades now of learning just how to really listen and make sense of information that is delivered faintly, quietly, or the symbols and pictures I often receive.

Communication either comes or it does not. I always tell my clients that medium type information is something I simply do not control.

THE ACCIDENT

A similarity between a Medicine Woman and a doctor is that we are both well-trained. A doctor, however, calls themselves a doctor once they receive a degree while I did not feel comfortable calling myself a Shaman or Medicine Woman until I was in my fifties. I had "walked the fire," so to speak, facilitating healing for hundreds, including myself.

This one night, I worked with a woman, Elizabeth, who was in her late thirties. She had two boys in their tweens. I would describe Elizabeth as quite pretty. She had a sweet demeanor and was soft spoken.

Our connecting that night began with her phone accidentally dialing me. I was taking my dogs out between clients and I answered my phone. I didn't hear anybody on the other end. With caller identification on cell phones, I knew it was her phone and I could hear people in the background. I thought, *perhaps, I'll text her. I haven't seen her in a long while. Maybe the Universe is prompting her to get back in for a treatment.*

So I did. I texted her similar words. She responded about some options for a session and we settled on night.

When she came in, I gave her a hug and she looked relieved to be back. I asked her what was new in her life and she responded with the basics: pretty much the same – kids, sports, and her position in the school.

Elizabeth had scheduled an hour treatment on the table. It was bitter cold and dark outside and I had the room warmed nicely.

I briefly told her about my two thyroid workshops that were coming up on how to notice thyroid issues and she indicated an interest to attend.

When we began, I asked if she had any concerns or requests. I also made sure she was comfortable. She related that she had eczema now on her eyes, mainly the left eyelid and on her left arm.

I asked her, "What is happening in your life that you do not want to see or look at? And, perhaps, more related with a female?"

"Nothing really," she responded, curiously.

I began our usual way with her on the table and using a simple guided relaxation: breathing deeply, releasing and relaxing the shoulders, back, the belly and so forth. A process similar to a yoga class. When I got to her left leg, I immediately saw the image of a brazen woman. One with bright red hair, the kind of take charge lady.

I tried to study her for a moment, this lady I was seeing, in my third eye center. During this, I attempted to continue to perform the bodywork in a fluid manner.

And then, the image was gone. I made a note of it and finished with the body and intuitive work as she had requested I work her feet really well. I could feel her exhale.

She came out of the treatment room to where I was standing by the counter and what a difference I could see in her. She was with a bounce again, looking joyful and ready for Friday at the school.

She paid and indicated she would text me again with the next time she can come in. I took the moment to tell her about the woman that I had seen, with the bright fiery red hair.

"She was a go getter!" I informed her. "Brazen, brash! I am curious how that relates to you?"

Elizabeth began telling me that she had numerous conflicts with a mother and particularly surrounding sports and the kids. "It causes me a lot of sadness and frustration and for the kids too!"

"This is the MindBody piece that is a part of my works as a Medicine Woman," I told her. "It is a larger part of the future works."

A part of this is to be able to educate the client about just what a Shaman does since they honestly do not know, and I am finding that because of my growing up perhaps somewhat differently, I had an expectation that most people knew of using intuition this way.

Elizabeth and I spent another half hour because I saw it as a bridge, both helping her and also broadening the acceptance in the community of Healers from the Root versus Western Allopathic Doctors. Each has its place and function.

I asked her, and I knew the answer inside: "Have you ever been bullied?"

She exclaimed, "Yes! Yes, I have!"

"And your parents, either one of them bullied in the past? Could you check if you do not know?"

I mentioned to her that as a Medicine Woman, I utilize the sensing equally and that we have these abilities located in the third eye center. I went on to explain that I look to the Root instead just treating her eczema or eye as a doctor may. I also often look to the ancestral issues presenting.

I am always in awe of how my guides and those of others bring to the table the necessary information from which we both benefit by being present together in this work. I began to share in a storyteller way, briefly, and it flowed:

"You see, my great, great grandfather was shunned from the family. He was African and I feel him. I have felt his pain, I hear him. He is a Guide for me.

"I realize this is unfamiliar territory, but he was shunned. Then my grandmother was left on the land, shunned when her mother died unexpectedly.

"My mother was rejected for all intents and purposes, being left at a care facility from near birth to a year of age before my grandmother came to get her in Missouri, a place I had to stop and do a meditation one year on a long road trip.

"I felt shunned by my mother on many occasions, and also that she is a competing mother. I just wanted to please her and I seemingly never could. Even when I reached the age of 53, we are disconnected completely. I had tried so many times.

"My son ended up with some issues and I feel in my heart that he may feel that I do not love him or that I shun him, yet, I love him more than I can possibly describe.

"You see," I continued telling Elizabeth, "the Ancestors' wounds are our wounds! Our wounds are their wounds.

"I am doing my best as a mother to circumvent those wounds from manifesting and redirect the family tree."

I shared with Elizabeth, "Please do the same. Contact your parents and ask them if they were bullied. And if they say no, understand that not always is it comfortable, nor could it be sequestered away as it was a wound, and people are not always comfortable talking about them. Please don't assume it wasn't there. Hopefully, Elizabeth, you will be given the information forthcoming."

I then addressed that this is the difference: intuition, MindBody, moving the stagnant energy meridians, and addressing from the Root. This is the difference between doctoring and shamanic guidance.

Elizabeth was very open, receptive and thankful for my gift of extra time and I was thankful to be able to showcase my intuitive works well within a subsection of a small conservative city.

I left and felt really good in gifting her the blessing as is always the case. I too was blessed by the meeting in a way I never expected. I was able to put words to my family dynamic, to what I learned from my grandmother's caregiver, who told me in no uncertain terms of our Ancestor that my great, great grandfather was shunned.

The Ancestors will lead you, guide you, if only you are willing to listen and be present and authentic. Be kind, be patient and listen.

Learn to hear them and practice it. You might feel like at first, you are grasping and not going to get it right, but, with time and a little practice, you will hear them. The lady that was the subject that I sighted with my Far/Third Eye had bright red hair. That was not a physical attribute. It was her hot temper.

CASTOR OIL PACKS AND FACIALS

I had a client one morning named Megan. I see her bi-weekly and when she first began coming for treatments over eleven years ago, along with her husband and many extended family members, it was primarily for fibromyalgia. She had also endured breast cancer.

Megan was highly intelligent, a former businesswoman, and an elder to myself. I respect her in so many ways.

She once told me, "I've never seen the colors before...like when you work on me!"

On this particular day, she had a ninety minute session at 9:30 a.m. followed by a Castor oil (Organic) Pack for her abdomen and liver health. She also scheduled a Natural and mostly organic facial, part of her Valentine's Day gift from her husband who takes good care of her!

I prepared an activated facial just before her treatment session by adding apple cider vinegar to a European clay that I had. I have about six types including some rare ones from Liberia.

During our session, Megan talked briefly and then was quiet for the remainder of our time, which is good medicine in and of itself. At first, when I was getting her comfortable on the table, I asked her if she had any requests.

"Could you focus on my right leg – the whole leg and the right foot?" she specified. She related several issues as she previously had a surgery that left her with quite a bit of scar tissue buildup on that right foot. In many of our session, I focus on it and rub it out.

During this session, I was working up the calves in front and I felt some major blockage that needed to be removed. At that same time, I then went down to the foot and she spoke out that she saw "flashing green and yellow lights" and then "the pain was gone!" I related shortly and sweetly that we had worked her liver and spleen meridians and those colors would be corresponding. Liver stagnation is often a pea soup green.

She loved the Castor oil pack for the liver and abdominals and she also really enjoyed the facial. She had the forty minute facial which allowed me to leave the clay on a bit longer since she chose to have the activated version. Her skin was just radiant when she left!

READING AT THE BLACK BEAR

One night, I ended up going to the Black Bear Casino buffet for dinner with my family. It is close to home and a rare treat. My son and his partner had flown in from Los Angeles, and it was a good outing to see the both of them and relax.

Anyway, we ended up waiting over an hour mostly in the lobby where they have big comfortable chairs. The two of them shared a chair in the main lobby while we waited for our table; the line was long. A guard came by and asked them to sit in separate chairs. We looked at each other, puzzled. They obviously fit well in the chair and were not hurting it, nor being disrespectful in public.

This particular security guard came up and commanded, "Young people you will have to sit in your own seat!"

At that time, I am sure she did not notice I was with them in my coat sitting on the other side. I watched as they separated and I asked my son, "What will be your response?"

"Oh Mom," he replied, "we will just move."

I decided to just get up and then walked around for a few moments and talked with a couple of younger staff members and they related that she seemed to be quite "bossy." About twenty minutes later, three Native team members came over and apologized.

"It was no problem," I replied.

One of the women asked if I was a Shaman and expressed her appreciation for the work we do. As we were standing there, near to the entry of the casino, I was looking at her face and I heard, faintly, the name Diane. I asked her about that specific name and she began to cry and hugged me.

She shared, "My mother passed twelve years ago. The name Diane was given as my middle name and was what she called me."

She went on to describe some issues related with her life and how she wanted to resolve them. That hearing from her mother like this just gave her tears and hope for feeling like her mother was a guide around her.

"Oh, yes!" I exclaimed. "She really is a guide for you! I heard her!"

The woman, fascinated by my knowledge of her mother, asked me if we could connect again, away from her job and we were able to discuss more details about her loved one. We wound up eating our dinner quite late that night before all going home.

Shamans have works or what most people call their vocation or jobs, which blend into our daily lives, a great portion of this is often unpaid. Our work is one of spirit, mental and also physical. Shamans are a combination of a medicine person, who possibly may also have any of the following attributes, particularly for their community: medicine people, warriors, guides or teachers.

In the world today, we too pay for our shelter, food, taxes, and living costs, and we must charge for our time, unless we have financial benefactors, which the majority of people do not. This causes us to charge either by the service we perform or by an hourly rate. But we still offer up our knowledge and information whenever possible to those we may come into contact with.

SHORT MEETINGS

My shop was temporarily closed when I had an appointment scheduled with Tracy so I brought my table to her home for her hour and a half session. We began around 8:00 p.m. Shortly after our session was complete, her husband, Stephen, came home with their dogs. Tracy asked me to chat with him briefly while she got dressed from her robe as she had just gotten off the table.

I introduced myself and learned that they were new to the area. Stephen mentioned that a family member of his was a Medium and that his wife told him that I often speak with and listen to those who have passed. We continued our conversation for about a half an hour before I departed their home. The works of Medicine people involves a lot of intimacy with clients and frequently with people we have only recently met.

For example, the following day while at the sauna, I was lying down on the top bench, meditating while my dreadlocks were soaking up some heat when a woman came in and was telling her friend, rather loudly, I might add that she kept having accidents related with her head. After much discussion, I chimed in saying, "You must be a Taurus."

"I am a Taurus!" she replied.

I told her, "Taurus' can be prone to head issues. They ram. They are the bull and are usually Earth elements." Earth is stable and, most of the time, dependable. It is committed and its structure is for us all.

Symbiotic Feelings

Holly, a returning client, came to see me for a treatment. She sent me a text and wondered if there was any chance to get in soon.

Before she arrived that morning, I began to have feelings which I quickly realized were symbiotic. I have learned now that with my clients, family, and even some folks I am connected with remotely, whether friends or those I have given readings and guidance to, I can begin to "feel" what they are feeling from a distance.

Holly came in the building ready for her treatment, smiling, and from the outside one could not tell she was hurting emotionally. She certainly hid it well. Before our session, she told me that she had pulled a muscle in her chest.

When we got to the table to begin our session, I felt that the sudden sadness that morning was mainly hers and we checked in briefly. She confirmed that she didn't really want the friends she had here. She wanted her friends back home. She wanted her husband home more as he was gone quite often.

In all my years of training in this area, I have the strength now and the awareness to decipher which feelings are mine and which belong to others outside of me and it makes me aware of our connections to one another and how we can begin to use this connection collectively.

SENSING FAMILY ISSUES

I wanted to share about a young man, Jermaul, who has come to see me a few times now. He was a beautiful, tall African man in his early twenties. The second time I had seen him, I remember the look on his face when he saw me play the drum that night. We were gathered around in my living room and the experience changed something in him. I saw it and yet even more strongly, I felt it.

Jermaul had several children despite being a very young male. I was happy to hear that he has made some very positive choices more recently.

He had only a partial payment but really wanted a session with me and I agreed. I wanted him to receive good body work and infused with love that I know he and anyone would benefit from. I also knew that he felt comfortable coming to me for body work as an African man.

I had been planning on going home when he called, but I agreed to come in a bit later. Before heading in, I went to the natural foods store and purchased two ginger beers and some nag champa to freshen my treatment room. When I returned to the spa, I handed Jermaul one to enjoy while I got the room ready.

As we began, I could tell he was looking forward and that just gave me the boost energetically to really also participate in his treatment. A call and response, if you will. Every drummer and dancer learns call and response and it is the same way with the facilitator of healing. You tune in to the client's rhythm and learn to follow the lead on where they need the energy and direction.

Once on the table and relaxed I began to work on his head, releasing mental tensions, giving him a meditative seed to relax and then moved to his chest and arms. When at his left arm, I found deep wounds from a female at the elbow joint. I slowly and carefully worked them, down to the legs and feet, and over to the other side of the body after he turned around.

On his right arm, I saw a characteristic shade of almost a neon blue. It was continuously moving and I remained steady while I watched it. I wanted to see what it would show me. It was like a line of blue, a very faint one, medium in size and I felt it was Father.

It is important to note that this particular shade of blue, usually in a line or squiggle, comes on a part of the body that is revealing and almost always shows mental instability or mental disease.

Through the session, he was often quiet and kept to himself, not sharing much of his personal and emotional self yet, preferring to radiate about a picture of his daughter.

At the end of our session, I related what I had seen. "There are wounds with female and grief. I also saw a man who moves with serpent energy, like a snake, who is watching you for an opportunity. And that you will not know who he is right now but you should pay attention. Also, there was a male with mental instability. Maybe he is losing patience with life? I felt as though it was your father."

I rubbed his head a bit longer and squeezed in on his legs and feet before I left the room, asking him not to rush, but rather to take a few deep breaths, and that I would meet him out there soon as he was ready.

Jermaul came and confirmed that this was all happening for him. I related that I wanted to be a Guide to help him with making good decisions in his life.

SEEING THE BLACK PANSY

Jillian had come in for a massage and was new to the practice but had heard about my abilities. She worked in an office that was near a few of my other clients, all of which had related what I had seen working with them.

Our session was quiet and in my third eye, I sighted a beautiful black pansy. I told her this as she was going to pay and leave, and she said she was going to get a black pansy tattoo that day in memory of her sister who passed. She was a new client and had never experienced anything like this before, having someone sense things about her. But she had been thinking of the pansy, obviously, and it was in the Field.

Sensing the Infection

I have seen her many times but on this day, Kimberly was experiencing a sore neck. I gave her both body work and an energetic treatment and when I got to her right foot, I sighted an image. There were microorganisms, round in shape, swimming in a liquid.

I asked of the Guides what this could be and they told me that she had picked it up from the water. I knew she had just returned from a trip to a nearby state and maybe she had picked up something. I later heard some recommendations from the Guides.

I asked Kimberly if she had been bathing somewhere foreign. She said she never does, ever, but she did at the hotel in Michigan. I went on to inform her of what the Guides showed me and the proper treatment to take.

"I just love you," she said, as she left the shop armed with information of her health.

A Mushroom Cloud

In the morning, Erica had come for a two hour session. She had been a bi-weekly client of mine, alternating 90 and 120 minute sessions for nearly eleven years.

She began to see colors when she first started receiving energy and body work sessions and we worked on reducing her discomfort related with a diagnosis of fibromyalgia and also stress. Erica was a woman I greatly admire and also deeply respected. She was always polite, well-spoken and courteous.

I had watched her consistently demonstrate quilt-making for those with cancer, be a dynamic grandparent and parent, and be an amazing friend to all, always consistent and conscious. A rare jewel!

In this session, she related that her neck and her feet were bothering her. I took loving tender care. In all the years of giving her service, I knew just what to do for her and I am always honored to work with her.

Yet, this time, I saw a large mushroom cloud when I got to her right shoulder. I almost forgot to share it as we were checking out after her treatment and she was rescheduling and paying for her session with me in the little sitting area to the side of the treatment rooms.

I mentioned it and asked her, "What do you think it may mean?"

"One of my sons is really struggling with finding a job," she told me. "Also, my husband is having some issues too."

There was much in the male area that was concerning her; although she would never feel to burden others with her concerns that way.

I have always done my very best to care for her. She is a true Empress. You see each person holds images, energy in the Field, and a person who is developed in the third eye chakra can sense and even intuit those images and then the other aspect of development is how to reason what the images may mean. Utilizing concepts I have learned in yoga, I have come to put the pieces together as to the side of the body and more.

A Visit to Intensive Care

I went to see a young man in the ICU by his mom's request. It was a Saturday morning and his mother requested I come as soon as I possibly could. Friday night, I knew I was too spent to drive to town and be on task energetically. So I opted for Saturday, as I would be fresh and rested.

It is interesting that I have many times been asked to go to Intensive Care at the hospitals and what changes have taken place today that Shamans and energy workers are welcome! You can do this work too – utilizing your heart center for the benefit of others.

I placed my hands on the young man's blankets which were atop his body and he was both sedated and with a temporary breathing assistance. His mother and others were worried that he would have to have some trachea work done and he was a vulnerable adult.

When she has brought him for many sessions to the shop, I have often given her information in his Field. He uses sign language which I do not know, but I can touch him and give her information about what he has eaten or events he has been on.

When he came in one week, I received information from him that he had severe stomach discomfort and had some gas and constipation issues. He confirmed to his mother that what I was relating was correct while he sat on the massage table with her behind, seated in a chair.

He has had issues with being physically agitated and never has had any issues with me. I see him as highly developed and sensitive and someone I can communicate with telepathically, when most no longer can.

The next day, following the energy work I did for 45 minutes at the ICU, the visiting mom said, "Wow, whatever you did…"

"What?" I asked.

She said, "Didn't mom call you?"

"No," my curiosity growing.

She told me he turned around completely. "The doctors are amazed! He's in another room out of ICU."

With smaller cities like this and coming here not really knowing anybody, talking, looking different and having some different ways, other people sharing about my work is what keeps me working and eating. Other people sharing the truths that I, myself, could not simply tell allows me to continue to help others, spiritually, energetically, and wholly.

A Case of Extensive Diabetes

I briefly had the pleasure of working with a lovely woman, Suzette. She had formerly been hit by a vehicle, and that caused the doctors to believe that her pancreas was no longer working. She had come to me for a table session, and I was able to glean some information which made the wellness consultation even more impacting, because her situation was such that she was injecting $20,000 in insulin per month.

This caused her hardened areas on her stomach and also affected her moods. When we first began our journey making food medicine, she was drinking large containers of soft drinks and I could see a real ruddy complexion on her face and could see that she suffered from frequent colds and flus, low energy and mood disturbances, given the drugs that the doctors had her taking.

I was so thrilled to help her and, for a few months, she did it! She used juice, smoothies, salads, lots of raw foods, and she completely changed. The weight dropped, the skin improved and she was using less insulin. The ladies at the pool at the gym where she was a faithful class participant made remarks that they wondered, "What is she doing?" She looked so good, vibrant and all!

But the foods today are powerfully addicting. This journey of food as medicine is a long journey for me – one over 30 years. I began with Pamela Masters in Los Gatos, California around 1989 in a raw foods training class, and other courses at Bread of Life in Campbell, California, learning from ladies who formerly were part of the "hippie" culture, who had super valuable nuggets to share. I kept a lot of those recipes.

I have taught introductions to raw foods, juicing, juice fasting, and many other classes and I incorporate this into the guidance of the wellness consultation. I truly believe any disease is curable. But two components are necessary: a will to live (motivation) and the ability to embrace and practice new ways (grit) and sticking to it, at least, for the goal.

I am going to share an important piece here as well: the body is very unforgiving when you return to the standard American diet (SAD) and begin eating what many teachers call the "blood and starch" diet. Animal flesh and rice and potatoes. Formerly known as the meat and potatoes diet. To go back to soda, all the sugar, pasta, is a hard thing for the cleansing body to return to. The body will take years to clear out the mucoid sludge that is built up in the bowel and deposits like kidney deposits in the urine and cleaning and clearing the lungs and skin.

The wellness consultation does not mean somebody has to be a vegetarian. I work with others who still want their meat or fish, and we find ways to add and not focus on subtracting. I do encourage strongly that people try to move away from dairy products due to the mucous production.

It was probably the mid-1980s when I began reading Arnold Ehret's book *Mucusless Diet Healing System*[7] about mucous and digestive issue and alkaline versus acid in the body. I use these teachings often in my current MindBody health.

THE GOLD BULLET — YELLOW FLOWER

I began the session with Kelly, a woman of her early thirties, with the usual dimmed lights, candle, warmed eye pillow and very soon after touching in, I see a brass or gold bullet. Then I saw a man in a uniform. The vision came and went quickly though.

Just before those two, I saw a yellow flower. It was a flower in memory, from long ago. Not mine, but hers. I saw an assortment of images but I also was getting that nervous feeling that she was likely born and raised here and maybe very conservative and not want to hear what I "see."

---

[7] Ehret, Arnold. *Mucusless Diet Healing System: Scientific Method of Eating Your Way to Health*. Ehret Literature Publications. 2011.

Kelly was receiving the two hour session on the table and that included a foot scrub and also a raindrop essential oil therapy on the spine. I thought I would wait to share about the bullet and the flower from her memory until after the reflexology.

When we were all through and checking out, we sat by the fountain in a private space. I saw the impact of the work upon her and it seemed her energy had seriously shifted. I sat, patiently waiting for the right time to tell her what I saw. You have to sense these things and find the invitation to address them, if you do at all.

So when I finally related my visions to her, and that what I saw, I sensed on her right, which meant for me that the issues were related to male or vocation, she indicated that she was quite angered with her father and he was formerly in the military.

I also related what that she was feeling stale, bored, and needed change and had no idea how to manifest that. It was a feeling as if she were internally speaking to herself, "There's no way out! This is not healthy!"

She paid and tipped for what she shared was a really appreciated service and I felt like some MindBody issues shifted for her that night.

After this session, I went back to the treatment room to clean up: blow out the candle first, strip the sheets, clean the stones, and such. As I was facing my treatment table and away from the entry door, I felt a definite finger tap me on the back, just above my bra strap.

I waited a moment as it was a female, for sure. I figured it was one of the gals at the shop asking me something, yet, as I turned around, I saw no physical person was there.

I truly felt like it was a sign from the Ancestors.

SENSING THE BRIDGE

Jackson was much like I am, yet younger. He was approaching his Fourth Moon therefore, he hadn't all the confidence it takes a Shaman in this realm.

He had perceptive abilities, for certain, and will develop his focus beyond where it is now. He was articulate, especially sensitive, and saw through the kind of lens that only "we" tend to look through at the natural world.

Before getting on the table, I asked, "Anything you want special attention with?"

"Yes. My neck and my lumbar spine," he replied.

That was about all he related, and I left, giving a few extra minutes for him to decompress on the warm table.

As I started our session, placing the warm pillow over his eyes ever so gently, I was aware of his innate sensitive side similar to my own. I dipped into the special oil I had made of coconut, cacao and others. It smelled so delicious; like that of chocolate. I immediately saw a few bridges and then those images passed. I then saw much smoke, billows of smoke. I saw some other images yet that I could not put to words for neither him nor I.

Seeing as how I was quickly approaching many images, I felt that I likely could benefit him by just slightly indicating what I saw at that time, and did my best to maintain the note in my mind, such that I would not forget them all. As I mentioned the bridges with him, he indicated he didn't know so I went on to the smoke.

I asked, "What is it that you are trying to see through more clearly? What bridges must be crossed?"

See, this is what I have been sharing with you here, that you learn, and develop the skill of how to relate the images. What to say and not to say. To be a Guide.

Once, I had related the images this way, he understood that it was about his life and employment and that it made perfect sense.

Later in our session, a large black bird showed up. It had protection around him and indicated it was staying on as a Guide in this lifetime. I assumed, given the size of this bird, that it was a raven. I related with him that I saw a raven, a rather large black bird, that was around him, and he in short summary told me of the crow, extra-large in size that had visited him on many occasions in the physical realm some time ago. He told me the meaningfulness of that which I sighted.

Lastly, as I was working with his cranium, I sensed some radiation issues on the right side of his head which are not uncommon.

With one of my clients who passed about two years ago, I was working with her and felt the brain tumor on the right hemisphere near to the ear. She was having a lot of headaches since she was in high school.

I now know what they feel like energetically. A healer would never, in my opinion, diagnose or make statements which would get us into trouble. I would never say you have a brain tumor. But, I would say, there are some issues here that I would be careful with radiation. You could get a protection device, or not hold the cell phone to that side of the head, reduce Bluetooth headset use, or suggestions of that nature.

In this case, I truly felt that the exposure was mild and I was able to help shift some of that energy asking him to do breath work with me, taking in some deep breaths and long exhales. What was formerly weakening his Field shifted dramatically.

I did ask him if he was using a Bluetooth device on that side and he indicated that he formerly held a job wherein he was required to wear a Bluetooth device and he was glad to be rid of it. Interesting!

As he came out of the treatment room, and I awaited just outside near the lobby, I noticed his pink cheeks and the new balance in his step.

READING ABOUT RELOCATION

Shannon's question was quite specific: Would it be in her best interest to let go, completely restart life somewhere else and have joy, health, and happiness and be financially better off?

I drew the card and received the following: Judgment, Strength, Seven of Hearts, Four of Wands, King of Hearts, and Nine of Swords.

The move would take place and she would use logic over intuition in the events to unfold prior to the move.

There is much to do to make it happen and she would make that happen.

There is pure and true balanced forthcoming love and energy in the life leading to success and there was a new chapter, if only she would no longer hesitate or doubt herself. She needed to successfully ask for help and get the matters going to facilitate the new chapter.

SENSING DEATH

When Matt walked into the shop for his treatment, I caught a hint of "it." He used the restroom, washed up and I, as I always do with my clientele, personally escorted him into the treatment room. At times, he would come more often than any of my other clients.

In this session, I could sense that there was a lot of trouble with his legs, and hips. They were wobbly. According to the MindBody aspect, this could represent a fear of letting go, having a leg to stand on, with a father predominately.

I came back to the treatment room to start our session. I began to sense it again, with my nose. That smell, at first, I notice it and then distinguish it from any other smells about me.

But in just a short bit, I realized what it was. The smell of impending death. Each one of us has a special note or signature.

I wouldn't have guessed it. He had so much and so many blessings. We talked of the future about which I consistently guided him, such as MindBody issues related to having a 'leg' to stand on with regard to business. I did my best to ease the distraction of discomfort in the legs created by the MindBody.

After he left, and I had cleaned the shop as usual, I went in, sat down, burned some sage and smudged all around the entry of my door as well as my table, the room, and myself.

I think that things are better now, and a solution may be found which is great. But I often share with clients that the MindBody inner talk that we all do must be clear, just as manifesting intentions are and when a person feels they have no way out, the body will provide an exit.

THE GOBLET

Deanna was a last minute call that day, and she was very thankful to get in for a treatment. I made her warm and cozy on a winter's night. I was not expecting to sight anything, but as she lay down, I placed a warm eye pillow from the linens heater cabinet that I have near my table, got her bolster comfortable under knees, and made sure she was comfortable with the temperature and that it was just right – a gentle fan in the background, a candle, soft nature sounds and music.

There we were, again, in the dance of life, two spirits working together, when I saw a chalice or a goblet. It appeared to be glass, etched crystal. Then I saw two, and they were then full of light and energy. A sight hard to explain in words. It was a third eye visual.

As I began to work down the body, I also remembered she had complained of fibromyalgia pain.

That blue that I typically see which indicates mental instability I saw going up her right thigh. Then, I heard a Guide say, "She wants out of her job. It is brutal on her nerves and spirit."

Yet, she had just come in so happy and bouncy looking and saying how she had the best job ever? She loved her job? She had even said she felt like she served God and helping people is her life.

What I saw you see, is that Deanna viewed herself as an "Angel." She specifically used that word. This is why in her Field, I saw the chalice or the cup full of light and energy.

People manifest the images pursuant to their own imaginations about life and life's expressions. Yet, she was in the MindBody realm, calling a way to get out of that job and for other reasons.

When I related that I heard that she wanted out, she began to sob. I stayed present with my energy and my warm hand on her back through the blankets, infusing her with love and comfort. Did you realize that many people do not have, and some never had loving, mothering types of touch? It can be very cathartic and healing.

She really began to cry and release all kinds of pent up frustration. She had stayed in that job and was overdue to get out. Today, she is like a new person in her strength and joy. She was always happy but today, she is really truly happy.

The other part of our work was that there were mounds of grief on her lung meridian of her reflexology points on her feet. *It must be hard to even walk*, I thought, working the hardened points on her feet.

I offered her a substantial discount to come back for an hour wellness and we would check in on an obvious thyroid issue, depression, anxiety, insomnia, cold hands and feet and sundry other issues checked on her health history, and that I would show her ways to up her glandular system and release some of that grief held in her lung meridians.

She was so thankful! She came out to pay for our session and told me it was the best she has ever experienced. That she just needed something for herself. The other therapist noted her buzzing with happiness and radiance. I think at times, they just watch for people to leave the treatment rooms, just as we do watching the ladies who leave noticing the before and after of their hair and nails.

One Woman, Much Suffering

Andrea had an afternoon appointment. It was the first time we had met. Another woman at the shop recommended my Shamanic services to her. Her friend met with us as well, a bit into the session.

Andrea related that she is Native American and she began to tell me of her roots, in large part Red Cliff. She said her line of people were, in her words, "hated."

As I began to touch-in with her and her Ancestors about her Field, I listened. I also perused the health form she provided prior to coming. I saw the strength, and I saw the trail of tears. There were so many manifestations due to fear, hurt and grief.

She presented with more symptomology and the doctors gave her many pills. In fact, she lived for months on a cycle of heavy narcotics, which she had just removed from her life only recently. She noted fibromyalgia, severe kidney issues, and a major hysterectomy.

After we touched in she began to explain the mutilation and it dovetailed with another piece I had been searching within my heart with another client. Andrea knew the details, and she spoke of it.

She said she no longer dreamed, that she drinks coffee all day, smokes cigarettes, and was giving thanks for her man that was concerned that she was cared for when he worked and was away from the home. She said that her partner's mother had a hate for Native Americans and that was a large problem in her life.

I began to sense her Energy Field as she was protective and highly guarded yet effuse with the share of her life. The foster home, the sexual abuse, the baby who was sewn to the outside of the mother's body. So many painful atrocities that happened with our Indigenous peoples. It is hard to imagine living through these, especially as a sensitive person.

First, I chose to honor her and to celebrate that which is her. To re-alkalize her body from the acidic heat. I start with listening to her share and honoring her, checking in to look into her constitution. It was strong, inherently!

How quickly we could transition her from the Neurontin and the statins which the doctors in their simple ignorance, prescribed and yet caused more problems in the long run. Most people are realizing about statin drugs that they are not the answer the majority of the time.

She had also experienced chemotherapy, surgeries and much more. I felt for her, for the emotional and other scars that were left the result of a lack of consciousness in a so many ways.

We did a nice rebalancing table session and also talked about diet modifications, like possibly replacing all the coffee drinking daily with some other options. You have to meet people where they are, and she was not in a place to make huge major changes given all she had been through, but starting with small enhancements would prove more successful.

SENSING THE LION

As my client, Jamie lay there, I led her into a meditative place to allow the MindBody-ism/schisms to release and free her mind. I visibly and energetically saw her body and mind relax and let it go. Working through layers of energetic body and also physical body, I relaxed a few key tension spots.

At the end of our session, I related with her about seeing a lion just after using the warm stones on her back. Sometimes I relate in the treatment room if it is busy outside in the lobby and I want to keep it private, as was this case.

I spoke softly that I had seen a proud lion and then some other assorted images, then a pink topped ice cream cone.

Also, I had removed an Energy Dart on her left side. Dart is a term I have come up with to describe over the decades removing stuck intentional pieces of projected negative energy, like a dart thrown at somebody. It was ascertained who likely placed that dart and she showed me some images on her cellphone after we met back up at the front counter following her session to reschedule and pay.

The lion was her recently passed Father. The ice cream cone, she related her favorite all time was cherry chip and she had been wanting one for the past three days trying to get to the local ice cream parlor in town.

The dart, she knew exactly who that came from and, was thankful as she felt it. She felt something there and was happy to have it removed.

THE 80TH BIRTHDAY TIARA

A client came, Beverly, whom I had seen for years. The year prior, in May, she turned eighty years of age. Before her birthday massage in the visit previous, she indicated she wasn't going to do anything special for her big day.

I went to our local dollar store and found a nice little birthday tiara and some Mylar balloons. She has frequently told me she had a rough marriage way back and the husband wasn't too sensitive to her or her needs. She never had children, and so I decided that had she something like this, with the floating balloons overhead and tiara, while walking home from the shop as she always did, she was sure to get some "happy birthday" greetings I knew she always wanted.

This last session, a year later, she had turned 81 and came for a massage several days before her birthday. I asked her what she had planned to do.

"Well," she responded, "I think that the two gals, whose celebrations I went to last month, may forget?"

"You know," I told her, "in life, we have to learn to make requests! I am no longer willing to be a victim to my expectations. Birthdays, or whatever, are important to me so I make a point to make a request. For example, calling a girlfriend in California or asking my partner to do something that would make me feel good. Often we have some emotional stuff behind it all."

I continued. "We are no longer victims just because we get sadness, anger or whatever other emotional baggage!

"I came from a home where it was not okay to talk about yourself at all, and I learned years later, I didn't really know myself and I had no comfort talking about my interests, accomplishments, and so forth. That's all changed now!"

Ladies, especially, do not let your birthday, anniversary, or any occasion, if it is special to you, if you have feelings behind it, go and feel upset or emotionally let down. Just make a request. Many of us look so forward to those Earthstrong/Birthday wishes on our Facebook walls, since most rarely send cards in the mail any longer. I have decided that one of these years I'm going to have a get together some place where others can meet up and just eat, drink and visit together.

Beverly and I had a good share about giving ourselves permission to love ourselves and make requests to be cared about or acknowledged on a day we may have some sensitive feelings. Everybody wants to feel safe and loved and feel a little special in their lifetimes. I learned from her every single time she came to the shop so it was a beautiful blessing to be there for her. She confided in me, telling me some of her very private life over the years and had indicated that she had never told anybody else. I believe that, considering how much I knew her.

A Reading to Prepare

I had not heard from Nicole in a while and when she sent a request for a reading, I was frankly amazed. She was an Apostolic Christian and I guess I always thought that was a particularly conservative church. I replied to her email and asked the amount of time she wanted to reserve for the reading.

She replied, "45 minutes."

Before she arrived, I felt a bit nervous, knowing she was a strong matriarch. She was accomplished and well experienced; an elder to I. She had seen much and traveled extensively. I felt also that her coming to me privately, as she asked for this reading to be, was a real testament to her attempt to conceal from the other ladies that she was a client of mine. She had been my client for massage and healing before, but I was now advertising readings.

She came in privately and she had trusted the years of information I gave her about the dairy industry and about what was good for her health. She used information I gave her with love, taking it to research it for herself and always came back and said, "You know your stuff, kid!"

I was honored she chose me for this work. I respected her and she knew the work I do is real. Though we do not see our spirituality the same way, I honor her for her choices.

As I pulled out the deck of cards and we briefly chatted, I used the exchange to pull into the energy of her higher self. She asked me some very personal questions and I witnessed her vulnerabilities.

For a woman who has manicured not only her inner garden but also taken meticulous care of her physical form, I sat up with the posture which was commanded by my respect for her. I was sure to pay careful attention to her words, her body language, and her eyes.

I began to sense just what she was asking. It was a multiple bridge of questions, leading the two of us in that treatment room with the tools present to the unfolding of her life's journey ahead, as we spent that time searching.

Yes, she had a good life and she had much to look forward to. A question about where she would ultimately rest once she moved from the area in which she currently resided. Many Elders do move from areas where they have considerable time to invest in keeping up their properties and she was not different in that respect.

When we finished, she looked into my eyes and I saw the answers she sought. I had passed on the information and she was thankful. She then gifted me with not only her payment but some interesting connections which was truly appreciated.

LETTING GO

She cried during the Guidance session and she cried tears of joy as we departed from the treatment room. There we sat, with a small table between Ruth and I while I splayed out the reading, eight ways.

Ruth carried survivor's guilt. She lived; he died. She was 18 and he was 20 when the car was hit and she was thrown. The next time she saw him, he was in an urn, never able to say goodbye in the flesh.

Now, married with young children, she knew no other way to let it go. She was going to marry him.

The reading revealed the experience did lend itself to strength in her current life and a strength she would not have had but for this truly moving experience. I asked her if she had another question. She said, "Did he assist in selecting my current husband?"

What was presented was uncanny: The Emperor and Two of Hearts. Based on this, I knew he was The Chosen One. Not unlike him. And a reversed hang man: "letting go now, living in the present."

What was most related was the intuitive pieces but the tangible is also moving for those who seek understanding of the ways of the Field even more.

I came into the shop the next day to find an envelope with some cash that Ruth felt to gift although, I know she's a mother with young children and I didn't ask for anything but a little trade on eyebrow plucking at the shop. She still wanted to gift it.

SEEING THE BLACK DOG

Last time Julie came for an Energy and Massage session, I saw a black dog that looked like a lab coming to her daughter. Part visual and part auditory.

I have never met her daughter and this client has come maybe three times; one of which was a wellness consultation.

She said, "Shaman, you know that black dog and my daughter you saw in our last session?"

"Yes, I remember."

"Well," she went on, "my daughter had a black dog that she is taking care of that she found. When I got home, she texted me a picture of it. It sounded so odd when you told me that, but just a day or so after, this dog is staying with us."

MOVING BLOCKED ENERGY AKIN TO A CYST

During my session with Michelle, I felt a blockage, similar to a small hard cyst on the right side of her neck. I felt it while keeping her relaxed and quiet. Then as I touched in, I felt it present with a reluctance to move. I began to visualize heat in my right hand and worked on the hard area on that side of her neck

Holding again for a moment I felt it "ready" and I moved it, flicking off the energy and physical body. As I did this, I saw a baby blue umbrella. I also noted what I have termed a "sodium rash" on her body.

I have found that people who unknowingly consume lots of bacon or sausage or Chinese foods and prepackaged foods get a tiny bump manifestation on the body. Once they allow the body to detox and move away from these nitrate and heavily salted foods, this goes away with changes of habit.

Michelle and I chatted a long while following her session. She discussed that she felt me remove the blockage and she then related that she perhaps wanted another child but that she went into early menopause at age 30. She had this confirmed with an FSH test by her gynecologist.

This is the misleading or incomplete information given to women which promotes a hopeless sense in people. Not a great way to be a healer in life.

I suggested that we do another trade or a few and that I could show her some ways to remedy this with diet and ways of living.

I believe she may have a boy in the future.

So Many Issues

Wendy was in the shop today, feeling a little sad. She related that she felt like her life was "down a hole, and she was trying so hard to crawl back up."

She asked if I could see her that day as I had agreed to take clients for another therapist at the Day Spa who was on vacation that week.

Wendy was in her early forties and I could see her protection mechanisms as I perused her health form, front and back. I saw a myriad of TMS (Tenso Myositis Syndromes) symptoms immediately. I caught on to the thyroid issues. When I questioned her about her thyroid and the Western doctor views, she said she had taken some thyroid medications earlier in life and then stopped and her levels were "fine" according to the doctors.

I asked the preliminary questions: Do you have cold hands and feet? I noticed her outlying eyebrow hairs were very sparse, and also asked her if she felt heart palpitations, or a "fluttering?" She was positive on all accounts.

Additionally, she had suffered endometriosis and that too caused my awareness of more potential thyroid issues. Years ago, people (at least here in the United States) ate a sandwich for lunch. We took a lunch to school and work and the bread was preserved with iodine which nourishes the thyroid. In Minnesota there is a deficit of selenium in the soil.

I saw her Third Chakra shining and I realized she was here for some work to get back up to speed. I asked her if the issues associated with this chakra were present and she said very much so. Money, relationships, marital stress, and she related that in her life, previously, she felt stressed watching her father beat her mother repeatedly and severely.

Wendy had cocooned herself into a protective state. She was so tight in her skin bag it was difficult to effect any change on her muscles. Yet she was mentally pliant.

I explained how Shamanic healing works and that, as a compliment, she could also come for a Guidance and Wellness session for one hour. The first time is a must to cover the ground we would need to.

When she set her appointment for Guidance and Wellness, we cover:

- How elimination functions
- Blood type
- Sex drive
- Sleep
- Dreaming
- What she eats
- What she likes to eat
- What her three primary goals are
- The benefits of juicing and how to juice

And so much more. Once you listen to the story each one has, you hear where the MindBody issues are manifesting and can move forward in addressing the myriad of issues.

Snow and Green Trees

A man in his fifties named Nicolas came to see me one day. He looked a bit weary from the toll of life but healthy overall.

We began in session as I always do: I light a candle, dim the room and ensure his comfort. Once I touched in, I was working on the right side of his head when he said, "Can we do an hour and a half?"

I assured him that we could.

I saw an image immediately of much snow and full green trees. I shared that and he related that he was a snow plow operator and formerly a logger.

Later towards the end of the session, in that quiet warm room, I saw an American Indian Elder which I asked him about.

He said, "No, I'm 100% Finlander."

"Oh, okay."

Later before he left he told me, "My sister did adopt twin boys who we now know are full Native American."

It is not everybody who is going to be open to this work. If I had not hundreds or so of confirmations of the images, symbols, and more that I see, I likely would not believe it myself!

This is the way: the Ancestors watch, they listen, they are always with us. We all are in the Field. I know, I hear them.

SEEING THE BLACK TALLY INK

Patrick's wife received an hour and a half session and then he received a two hour session. He had problems with numbness in his right arm. When I began to work the right arm a bit, I could sense the discomfort he was feeling. I applied some aloe, deep heating rub and sitting on my stool I released "heart protector" on the pericardium meridian. I learned about this from all my sessions for myself at Five Branches[8] in Santa Cruz, a Traditional Chinese Medicine school and clinic.

I cleared out where I found restrictions. It was highly involved and took much mental strength as well as physical application.

Then, I saw the image – a black ink tally and I saw a red line. I heard the new vehicle is offsetting his financial goals.

I related with Patrick about what I saw and he confirmed that it was bothering him a bit. I had no idea, but

---

[8] "Five Branches University." http://www.fivebranches.edu/

the right side (male/work) and arms (mobility/reaching) and black tally, keeping the budget balanced and the red, out of balance, was the Root cause in the arm pain.

After reading Dr. Sarno, I noted that we both, in the work that we each do which is complimentary in the area of MindBody, realize that when you relieve a person's mental stress, you end up also relieving their physical pain. This is because, as Dr. Sarno states in his book as an M.D., pain is caused by an oxygen deprivation. When the mind is stressed, the body will begin to tense and the tension syndrome manifests in a predictable area of the body.

Patrick related with me that he was concerned about a new vehicle purchase and the impact on their finances. While he liked it, and wanted it to help his wife feel "safe," he was also going to have to work longer before they could retire.

This client and many of my other clients are 'regulars' and they have attended some of my classes and we have discussed my works. When new clients have asked, I share the following:

"I believe these developed gifts are in part, in my blood; were a part of my upbringing; and a continuous path of development in the over 50 years of my life. I see them and helping others to develop them, as paramount to our survival as people on planet Earth; to be able to sense, and utilize our inner guidance and protection systems.

"The other piece that I bring is that with a new way of living, making food our medicine, we progress into a civilization that values real and fresh food. That becoming our standard and not the processed and chemicals of today also decrease the warfare, turbulent emotions, and lack of focusing."

An interesting note I wish to share is that people become less anxious, depressed, have far fewer visits to the doctors, take fewer medications, and are more productive when eating a whole foods diet which is also a benefit for the carrying capacity of the Earth today. It is also less of a burden upon our waterways with fewer hormones and drugs being excreted through urine and into our ground water both, by factory-farmed animals and people.

This also reduces our social services systems burdens, managing people who are often with mental health issues. While I cannot say as to everyone's situation with mental health issues, I am aware that if you detoxify, and return the body to a state of balance, many of these issues simply no longer are a problem. That alone is of huge significance.

Large parts of my journey included personal healing and I found through exploration: massage, Ayurveda, herbs, cannabis, cleansing internally, raw and vegan foods, acupuncture, reading, walking, exercising, drinking clean water, visiting the ocean, and having friends all very important to the journey of life.

I would receive acupuncture at the Five Branches Institute in Santa Cruz, as I worked to release some issues with myself for a number of years. I had some regular liver and spleen work and also scalp acupuncture. When I was "needled" by interns and doctors at the clinic, I was often able to name the colors of the meridians at the needle site.

I remember one intern I worked with went to share that with the doctors as the meridians all have a corresponding color. I learned of the pericardium points with receiving work in that area of the body, and that knowledge is something I bring to the table in my practice through exposure and feeling the benefit. The needle points have a corresponding number, but I remember a few interns using names like "heart protector" and "heart shield" and through using these services I also bring that into the table work I do for clients.

SENSING ALASKA

I walked into the shop where I rent my business space and a woman was seated receiving a pedicure. She was a young Native American woman and had seen me once before, long ago. Likely in her early thirties, she was just radiating, and I then felt the pause to stop a moment.

I heard inside my third eye center, "Alaska," and I came inside in that quiet space and I asked: "what about Alaska?"

I could not just blurt that out, so I made some idle conversation, like asking if she was from here.

She replied "Yes, all my life. Well, I lived in Oregon for a few months. I love it there, in Oregon. I want to move back!"

"Yes," I agreed. "I love the west coast. I am hoping to move back or spend a large amount of time there."

I then found a segue to insert what my Guides had shared and I said, "You have Ancestors in Alaska." They told me to tell her that she will meet her ancestors in Alaska.

At that moment, both of the ladies giving pedicures turned with their mouths open and wide-eyed as the woman, stated: "I am leaving for Alaska tomorrow!"

Apparently, before I had come to the shop, she was telling them about how she was leaving for Alaska the next day.

Again, this often causes some people who are more conservative-minded to be cautious or afraid. They are not sure what is happening.

This young woman shared with me that she was hoping to be able to move to Alaska in the future and that she felt a special pull to be there. She smiled and said, "Shaman, I will be back in to see you when I am back home to Minnesota."

Jungles, Rainforests and Bengal Tigers

A clean cut kind of guy, I could tell he had ancestors from other parts of the world as he carried a bit of an accent.

I reviewed Tom's health history sheet – perhaps a few TMS issues, some mild stress issues – nothing too severe, on paper anyway. He was somewhat anxious for sure. His partner had shared with him that I "see things" and I think he was a bit worked up. I have later since learned that he is very unfamiliar with intuitive wisdom and that also presented some anxiety as well.

However, some males carry a little bit of anxiety. In today's world, there is an anxious feeling when they are undressing, getting on a table and having another woman touch their bodies.

Tom settled in with some guided relaxation, some yoga type relaxation cues for the chest, the throat, releasing the belly, and allowing the body to become soft and relaxed; allowing the mind to also just relax and not be in a going or doing mode.

Very soon after I touched in with his head, I felt an irregular cranial shape and realized that he had had some cranial surgery early in life. Very soon after I began to see in my third eye some trees. They were white as if birch bark, then quickly the images shifted in my third eye. I saw tropical, lush, thick, rainforests, and then a Bengal tiger caught me by surprise. It looked right at me!

This was indeed a bit different.

Next on this journey, I was watching a blue shape similar to a jellyfish, kind of pulsing under the veil of his cranium I had no idea what that was.

And, I want you to know that you will not always know what all the symbols you see mean. You just won't.

I began to get some other images, but first, his mind was still a bit active. You can tell because the eyes are moving under the eyelids.

"You have an affinity for tigers and lions?" I questioned.

"Oh yes, tigers!" he responded.

"What about trees and tropical jungles and rainforests?"

He kind of shrugged, signaling it did not click for him.

As I got to the right side of his chest, I received the images of dirt bikes or railers or something that had caused some issue with the congestion I felt about his rib cage, and when I related about that he indicated he used to spend a lot of time on ATVs in the dirt.

There were a few more, but lastly, I received an image of two ladies in a black and white type of photo, yet they were slightly animated. They were currently Guides in his life, from father's side. I asked if he had seen their photo. He indicated that he believed he had seen them. I was unsure of the time period. Given their attire, it was likely 1800 or maybe even earlier.

I later learned that this client had an alcohol problem and was arrested. This could have been the image I saw in his brain area. I will not truly ever know, but it is good to consider that may have been what was happening.

LOSING ONES WE LOVE

It had been a long time since I had seen her. When Gail came in for a session, I first began to relax her then work on a uterus point that felt blocked which I released for her.

On the flip side, cleaned out her shoulders with therapy using some slightly deeper tissue work (carrying a burden) and removed a few blockages (not common) that were there.

I saw her Energy lift!

At the end, I used very warm stones across her back, some work on her spine and immune system near each vertebra, and I placed some into her palms as I touched in my hands on top of each palm/stone for just a moment.

After I exited the treatment room, I washed my hands and wrote down a few notes from our session for her on a return appointment card. She came out of the treatment room beaming! She related that she "felt so much better!" She shared that since her husband had passed, and the anniversary was approaching, she continued to see "black birds," "large black birds" and felt it was him around her. She asked if that could be possible.

I indicated that it surely could. The living natural world is a synchronistic living being that shares life with us.

We talked about the throat chakra center, "speaking ones higher truths," and how I saw the strong blue colors bleeding through into higher chakras. How I relate that this is a positive sign in the Field showing that her strength was moving up the spine towards the crown chakra and gifting her with being able to speak her values and insight in life.

I stress not putting a definition on all that I see with clients as it is a gift for the recipient to take and usually find the meaning or definition for themselves. Often, later they discover the significance of that message that I showed from their Field.

Gail shared how she was feeling really great and stronger in balance and, the last thing we reasoned about was our "Moon cycles" as people and the significance of the changes; some of which are predictable given a certain moon period.

THE LEDGE

I had a session with a business owner, Gerald, who I used to see regularly and, on this particular day, I saw a ledge. It was interesting because I may not have deciphered "ledger" but I was first shown in my third eye a "ledge" like a dirt ledge and then the transition was made to ledger. It was interesting how that leap came about. Staying fluid and present is a key! Almost like a stepping stone reading, where you get part of the word like *Jeopardy* or something.

Then, I was shown an image of black ink, just a spot of it.

Out loud, I found myself saying, "The ledger is in the black?"

It was on his right shoulder that I was working while he was face up, eye pillow on. Again, the right side relates to work and male issues.

"You're good!" Gerald replied.

"It seems with the image on your right, that you must have corrected or fixed something?" I continued.

Again, he exclaimed, "Wow!" and he went into a quiet place.

I thought, *I was not sure if I was on it or not.* You would think after a lifetime of doing this work I would always be sure of the links, but I am humble and I, too, can wonder if I get what I see correct at times.

As Gerald came out of the treatment room and into the shop lobby where I was seated and waiting, he paid and said, "That was really something!"

I related that he is easy to read because he is open, thus his Field is also open.

When he first started coming to see me for therapy it was for his legs, one of which was run over as a child, and I began to reintegrate the energy equally in both legs. I also moved the strong smell he was carrying as well as the lymphatic congestion that was rather intense. During one of our earlier sessions, I had seen a broken tree branch. I again, saw it on his right side and heard some information. He was relatively new to my practice and related that things had broken off with the family and his brother had called and was interested in meeting up with the family. He indicated that his brother was always very intuitive, but really struggled with some mental health issues and moods.

I shared with him that the majority of us who are deeply empathic, clairvoyant, clairsentient or clairaudient to a high degree are not easy for sure! But that often, residing in the Great Lakes Region around Michigan, Minnesota, Wisconsin and the outlying areas were known to be hard areas to live with. There are a lot of issues like this and they were often, not always, related to the thyroid gland disturbances and for sundry reasons.

People are not always going to be open-minded, but with kindness and love, some will get there! Some will be interested enough to listen, make changes, perhaps even save their or somebody they love's life. Then, it is where our change as a whole ratio reaches critical mass and great change can be made!

THE FENCE, THE TUDOR HOME

Clara had booked an hour and a half and then converted her session to a two hour session. She had a special request: lots of abdominal work. She knew that her center was compromised. She also had experienced some surgeries and that, too, was an issue she talked about.

She works in the medical field and she is very high strung, also having a thyroid issue that is not properly dealt with. It manifests in no sex drive, thinning hair, and metabolic issues. She was like I had been, eating to keep up her energy.

As I worked her core, several images came up: a fence and a Tudor home. I would proceed down that path and we would explore that, as she was talking during this session.

It was interesting, but she related she was saving for an extensive fence to put around her country home, for the dogs mainly. She was in the planning stages of figuring out the finances to be able to do it about six months from that time. The Tudor home was a dream home of hers and likely sensing this in the Field had everything to do with her holding and preparing for these things in her energy.

ROOT TO CROWN

Lynn indicated that her sister and she had some recent problems. When she was face down on the table, I was drawn to an area of her spine. I put my finger there and indicated it was a spot she may want to seek chiropractic help for as to her alignment.

At the end of our session, I energetically removed some blockages. She had requested that I work with her chakras and specifically if we could do a guided visualization, which I was delighted to do, Root to Crown, and found where it was originating, moving it back into place. I never took a class on chakras. I intuitively knew to use the palm of my hand over an area of the body and I can actually feel them, and often feel heat or coolness in their region of the body as well as sight images or colors.

Lynn related that she also liked the Narayan gel I used and the smell of it.

FINDING HER MAN

We met at a local restaurant, each had a salad in the bar area and then we went to a quieter booth and got cozy. Then Dalia asked me her question: "Will I meet a handsome man in, say, the next three months?"

"Well, let's do some clear manifesting together." I took a piece of blank paper out of my folder and handed her a pen.

"How about we make this fun and write down what you really want in a partner or man."

She wrote and together we got her ideal man down on paper for a visualization and manifestation.

I suggested she go to the local dollar store and get a nice 11 by 17 poster board, the color of her choice, and some colored pencils and do it up nice! Make it fancy and clear and then copy the list at her office tomorrow and put one in her car. I told her, a couple times per day to review it, dream it, be it.

We then drew cards. Of the six cards she drew, five of them were hearts, along with the Justice Card (reversed).

She's waiting on a grant, she said.

Basically, her list was for a tall Native man, 43 to 55 years of age, intelligent, motivated, likes nature, non-drinker, smoker, light herb smoker, and financially stable. It seems that she has the potential to meet a man with some, many or all of these attributes at a family reunion or function within the next three months.

I asked her to draw a circle on her art she would make and to have the four directions with her 'animal' in the center (power).

She indicated she is from Crane Clan but is unsure if she is Eagle? We finished up by discussing how she could find her own power animal.

THE BEAGLE

Craig was a large, gentle man who coached and had a lovely family. His wife and daughter also occasionally come to see me for natural wellness. On this particular night, Craig had reserved a ninety minute session.

During our session, I kept seeing in my third eye, a small little beagle. I had to ask: "do you have a dog?"

He replied: "Yes."

I said, "Why do I keep seeing a little Beagle?"

"We have one. It's old and senile."

Later, I saw this fiery cauldron on his left mid back. This was the same area he had pointed to when he arrived as an area to work on.

Left, as you remember, is the female or mother side, and I knew this was arising as a female related issue in his life. Sure enough, it was a conflict with a female "boss," he said, and his "ex."

"It must be somebody you view as a bit of a 'witch?'" I joked.

We laughed, because laughter is great medicine!

Sensing a Metal Instrument

Emma called me asking for a session, saying she needed to just relax and get some therapy. Once she arrived, she indicated that she was struggling with a partner. During our session, I saw a metal instrument. I could not quite make out exactly what it was in my third eye center.

What is this? I wondered to myself.

I then saw more clearly it was like a large trap. A bear trap, perhaps?

At the end of our session, just before finishing, the room was dark and she was well relaxed,

I asked, "Can you repeat after me please?"

"Okay," Emma agreed.

I said, "I am not trapped."

She repeated it and then burst out sobbing, releasing the tension she had long been holding that was so stressful.. She said it again and I asked her to use her "angry voice" and let it out! I felt as if she had more to let go, more to release, and she did use a more powerful voice than the softer, still seemingly victim voice I had experienced in that room.

She had some homework for the next two weeks before I saw her again to repeat that mantra as many times per day to herself or out loud as she felt necessary. "I am NOT trapped!"

Once out of the treatment room, she said, "We just had that conversation last night and that word 'trapped' must have been used during the majority of it."

"I don't know how you do this," she continued, "but I deeply appreciate you. Please don't ever move."

I took that as a compliment.

ROOT OF THE PROBLEM

Often times, people will go see a doctor for an issue that is troubling them. It could be dizziness, headaches, bowels, stomach problems, skin issues, depression, anxiety, ear problems, and more.

In this case, a woman name Crystal sent me a text relating that she was feeling "lightheaded" and "dizzy." When she arrived, I asked her if she was feeling any better. She related that she had gone to the Urgent Care Center as she had "blacked out at work."

She was obviously sharing that she was scared at the visit to the hospital in town. As a result of previously being diagnosed with "deep veins," the technicians were using an ultrasound to check for what may be the issue for these symptoms she was presenting with. They used ultrasound testing, took numerous blood tests, CT scanned her lungs and chest and when she came in, I saw the numerous bruises evidencing the trauma she had experienced while being poked and prodded to check the status of her body.

They sought to rule out a lung embolism, a virus, or something else. And, as a consumer purchasing services from a hospital or doctor, you and I would be very nervous given that she was experiencing those symptoms that she shared she was experiencing.

But what if hospitals and clinics had Shamans on staff that also visited with patients? We would ask the questions that would likely avoid some of this testing which is also a detriment to the consumer.

As Crystal was on the table, she was sharing this experience in our one hour session. I realized she likely had some thyroid issues (most do), likely also some candida (due to her admission of chronic alcohol use) and then, also likely parasite imbalance due to the Candida Albicans.

I asked a couple simple questions: What different items had she eaten the day or two before this incident? Had she consumed some sugar items?

She related a resounding "yes!"

She said, "I and my daughter went to Coldstone Creamery and had some ice cream. It's rare that I have dairy and sugar like that."

"And how did you feel soon after eating it?"

"I felt kind of warm and low energy," she answered. "And later the same day, lightheaded. But the next day was so much worse!"

What a simple fix to have had somebody who could have spent only five minutes in a non-critical situation to help with guidance work.

This is the work of the Shaman, in part.

Crystal was relieved to know that the medical system did not find anything and that likely her pre-diabetic diagnosis and this consuming ice cream with dairy and all the other sugars, did likely cause the fairly common spike in her glucose and the resultant Candida Albicans reaction.

So many times, when people come in for sessions either energy work and massage or wellness consults, just a clarification of their diet will produce large change. Eliminating foods that are causing problems and concentrating on using foods and increasing food as medicine will also bring about positive change, often in terms of weight loss, better eyesight, better hearing, better focus and general overall better health.

I love to get people started on green smoothies, salads, juicing, and introducing them to making healthier selections, like using nori sheets in place of bread. Since being raw foods trained in 1989, I have watched the whole raw food movement spring, with many making entire businesses and supporting their families selling superfoods and dried raw foods, like persimmons, mangoes, dates, and all were main staples in the diet of those long ago. Nut butters and seaweeds and all the good stuff that keeps us so strong and vibrant!

My Dear Brenda

Brenda came to me as a client though her husband, who has written a beautiful reference to my work. She came for over ten years, first coming to my shop and later, I would drive to their home. Dale brought Brenda with a pseudo dementia diagnosis and later was identified as Pick's Disease.

Brenda's brain had issues as a result of this and within six months of our doing energy work weekly, the scans which were done at that hospital showed a halt in brain deterioration. Dale came back and let me know that doctors had told him that they did not have any idea how energy workers do this, but they have it seen several times and for some reason it works.

Dale was always so appreciative of my work and often gifted me with beautiful jewelry, natural soaps, and fresh country apples. You cannot imagine how much I appreciate that thoughtful kindness, as a single mother and small business owner, I did not have extra funds in our budget for a chance to get away most of the time in the harsh winters, nor for jewelry. He really brightened my spirit.

Weekly, I would come to the house and do my very best to make Brenda comfortable, gently stretching her, talking with her, giving Dale insight about her health, about things to do to make it easier for her, some health tips, and more.

Brenda passed a little over a year ago and I knew that with already losing two children of their four and now his wife, it was going to be brutal. Despite our lifestyles being very different – myself coming from California and Dale being from the country in Wisconsin – I truly love this family. I learned so much about many things from Dale; I will always treasure that time well spent with him and Brenda.

I was at the hospital when she was admitted at the hospice and also attended her funeral as I have done for many of my clients over the years. This is a part of the Shaman's path.

OIL PAINTING AND BEAR PAW

Abby arrived one morning, delighted to be at the shop again. It was her second time. Once on the table, she was expecting only to relieve her body and prepare her for the upcoming local marathon.

I placed a warmed eye pillow on her. She was rather high strung, likely at that time, due to some issues in her life, as many of us can be at times in our lives.

I began to sense from my third eye very soon after I touched in and I saw a distinct oil painting of the Sun. Next, working on her right arm, I saw the lower arm or paw of a bear. After her one hour session, I brought up what I had seen. I related that she has "bear energy" and that the painting may have been our "want" for the Sun?

What was interesting was that I also saw a Native American man standing with a full headdress; a man of power, by the way it felt sensing him. I related these images and Abby began to cry a bit. She said that she had so many Native American things in her home, that she was always attracted to them for some reason.

It was awhile later that she contacted me and was suffering from shingles. Now, if you strictly viewed this through a typical western allopathic lens, you would see an event of shingles just hitting an individual. Yet from my perspective, the bear paw I saw was a warning that she was going to be slammed with something and I had given her some wisdom of this. When we worked together on the shingles issue which was quite debilitating, she was off work over a month and then took her retirement soon after feeling better. She was on her way to a higher education.

In our wellness work, I had her juice and get onto some powerful foods like camu camu, and she really pulled up, as she could barely drive herself to meet me for our appointment initially.

Camu camu for those who do not know is a powder, made from the camu camu berry which is sun dried ideally, or kiln dried, and used in water or drinks as a potent food-based form of Vitamin C. Great for the tissues and also complementary for a detoxification, which she needed to do, for both mind and body.

SENSING THE ELDER WOMAN

Sofia had been coming weekly for a while, taking care of herself. During this specific session, I saw little white flowers down her left arm. They looked like apple blossom flowers.

I asked her, "What are the little white ones this time?"

She replied, "Oh, those are not my favorite. I had to work them most of the day, removing the little dead ones from baskets."

Then, a woman with a blue/green or teal colored long dress that looked like a nightgown appeared. A true elder, a much older woman, and she just stood and looked at me while I worked with her energy. She stayed maybe a minute total and she faded away.

I shared this with Sofia and that she was on one particular side of her body, meaning perhaps from a particular side of her family.

What was interesting was that she was working with flowers in a greenhouse nursery during the day as a temporary job. They were in her Field.

INFERTILITY WELLNESS

Rosanna asked for both a table and a wellness session and explained her investing about $27,000 in infertility treatment to be able to conceive a child.

Once I was working with her mind, body, and spirit, I noticed the extensive lymphatic issues. I asked while she was on the table if she eats cheese. She related that she loves cheese and, I talked about that clogging her system and creating mucous in the body, being a factor in her obtaining fertility.

Cheese today, has everything to do with arthritis, cancer, and all the aches and pains of the stiff morning body from waking with a body full of congestion due to mucous.

Rosanna told me that her partner eats a block of cheese in one sitting. I asked if he possibly already had any arthritis and she confirmed, unsurprisingly, that he did.

I gave her some good lymphatic work on the table and then we progressed to the wellness consultation as she wanted both the same day. Talking about the impact of the diet, MindBody, exercise, and thyroid issues, about living in our area especially and thyroid issues and ways to handle that, and improve the glandular system.

These consultations are to lift people in ways that the physician in large part has not invested the thirty years I have in learning natural remedies and cannot have the time for. It is not their "domain."

As I ended the session with Rosanna, I did a brief chakra balancing. I sensed issues in the second and seventh chakras. I asked her: "Are you angry with yourself?"

She replied that she was. She paused and I waited, holding my hands over her heart and head until she exhaled, holding a space for her to be able to release some of this.

REMOVING ENERGY DARTS

While on the table, Jacob related that he could not move his neck properly and it was impinging his shoulder He was sure he injured it in a snowmobile accident recently. As I worked with him, I found two "darts" which I had not expected, as he is quite a fair person and gives a lot. I located and removed the darts and energetically swept away that energy from the body.

I asked him to lift his arms while on the table just before he was to turn over and he was able to with ease.

He left the shop with a big smile and a thank you, as well as offered a generous tip.

Upon leaving, he asked "Who gave me the darts?"

"I don't know, I'm *only* a Shaman," I joked. We laughed and gave thanks.

Later he texted me, "I get the darts!"

I replied "Bless."

GROUNDING AND REPLENISHING

In all my years as a Facilitator of Healing, I have always communicated the MindBody link to whatever ache, pain, or disease is manifesting for the individual.

One night, a woman, Eve, came in and asked for an hour session. I had seen her once or twice before a couple years prior. She had heard from many friends of hers that I was their Shaman as well.

Eve was so anxious to receive a reading. I shared with her that many times I would love to receive something for an individual and often I do not. A majority of the time, when I spend this time with the client in a massage session I can read in the physical realm, even if not the spiritual. I go into a meditative state as I have for years on a daily basis and work with the client's energy.

Eve asked twice in our session to please give her a reading and I began to wonder if I would get anything. In our session, I sensed enormous grief. I saw beautiful purple colors about the third eye and crown chakra areas and then sensed a crescent moon at her feet. When I began our session, I placed a warmed eye pillow and gave her a relaxation statement to breathe in deeply and allow her spine to relax.

I was guided to offer soothing and grounding work as she was wired to the max! Her mental realm was overworking. She presented with a right ankle issue which likely was related to something with work and having a leg to stand on with her job.

I feel I was divinely guided when communicating with her following our session. I told her, "I have offered grounding to settle your adrenals and mental realm. You are overworking your thought processes with 'task orientation.' There is substantial grief and it brings you to this 'task orientation' in almost a religious way of continuing to be on task and not let your guard down. This has physically manifested in these atlas shoulders with bands of burden. Your crown chakra colors are present showing a close connection to what you view as God. There is a crescent moon at your feet which shows me you wish to be more present in the mystic and Intuitive world, but there is fear to do so, it lies at your feet, awaiting you to walk in anytime."

This is the nature of my daily works. A Shaman is a giver of life, a holder of those who will pass into spirit yet once again, a nurturer of the Divine.

I have shared these short pieces of the hundreds of clients which I helped along their journey in life; in the majority they are anonymous so as to protect private details. I never planned for my life to be exactly this way, and I heard, far too often, that I was "eccentric" or "esoteric" and all forms of setting me apart and different. Yet the truth is, if I can do this and sense as I do, there is something greater that we all can do.

I am determined to present that as an option, one that I choose to plant and grow from a seed to strong tree!

I waited a long time in Cloquet, Minnesota feeling very different; it brought about anger, anxiety, depression, and I watered my garden of knowledge while I was here because it was all I really could do in a small town – parent, study and contemplate.

I realize that there are many small towns in America, and that there are enough of us who prefer to live simply on this Earth and value partnership models over dominator models. I give thanks for reading Riane Eisler around the time of her beautiful book, *The Chalice and the Blade*[9] and for Lillian Roybal-Rose[10] for the impact of her Cross-Cultural Communication workshop that lasted days at Cabrillo College. For my beautiful Guides and Ancestors who always showed up and carried me despite enormous hardships, you made my load softer and sweeter. You knew I was truly alone in this world.

And, I thank you for taking your time to enjoy my journey.

I genuinely see the Field and communicate with animals, I get video clips of events, feel things in a heightened

---

[9] Eisler, Riane. *The Chalice and the Blade: Our History, Our Future.* San Francisco: Harper Collins. 1987.
[10] "Lillian Roybal-Rose." http://roybalrose.com/index.html

way. I am extremely sensitive in a different way. Foods can really be empowering and also very disabling for me.

I know one thing: Everything is, Everything!

One love!

Shaman

Your Side of the Table

"I have had sessions with Shaman since early spring of 2010. In one of my first sessions, while being treated, Shaman had a strong feeling- sense there was an unidentifiable 'spore' in my bodily system. She explained to me she does not offer medical diagnoses but gently suggested I needed to have it checked out. She recommended at the time a holistic chiropractor in the Walker, Minnesota area, whom she felt could provide an interpretation, if I wanted to remain on a homeopathic path, or my primary physician; I took neither routes and later that year in October I had been diagnosed with breast cancer.

"We are normally quiet in our sessions, in large part, however that day she interrupted the session as she was 'told strongly' to Guide me in that way. I have knowledge that she is Medically Intuitive with others and myself and has given, known to me, Shamanic Guidance that includes: clairaudience, clairsentience, and clairvoyance.

"I attended one of her 'Free Skool' sessions in October 2013 where she gave back to her community. This is a community she has raised her son in, operated a business as a Shaman, and conducted practices mainly in the area of bodywork/massage; for years it has been known to her clientele that she gives her guidance and impressions offered from the Field, as she puts it.

"At this Free Skool a gathering of nearly 30 women and 2 men came together. She showed us how to do free readings for ourselves and explained how she had developed her intuitive abilities over the course of over 40 years, afterwards she had prepared food and invited everybody to eat and socialize together.

• • •

"I occasionally bring my son, Kayne for treatments with Shaman. He loves going to her and loves her massages. Although, he has some medical and neurological issues she is able to communicate with him and help him as he must take drugs prescribed by Allopathic physicians, some which help and others which also create tension for him both psychologically and physically. Karen has touched his hand and has been able to relate with me details of his life that may include: what he is thinking, what he ate, and/ or things he has experienced; my son has affirmed these telepathic communications by his use of sign language

"Most recently, in August of this year- 2014, I placed a call to Shaman on a Friday afternoon, August 23, and asked if she could come to do 'Energy work' for Kayne at the ICU unit at St. Luke's Hospital in Duluth, about 17 miles away from her home, due to he had been hospitalized 5 days by then for double pneumonia and no progress was being made medically. She immediately contacted me ready to come to our aid and a date was set up for the next day Saturday August 24. She arrived, not only because this is the way she makes a living but because of she wanted to help Kayne in this time of need; she also help me- went an extra distance without charging travel time.

"At that time Kayne had been incubated from August 18 – August 23, sedated, placed on breathing assistance equipment that worked his lungs for him and also protected actions that could have shut his heart and organs down. Following Shaman's 45- minute 'Energy session' a noted improvement began that evening, the next day he was

\bullet\ \bullet\ \bullet

allowed to be weaned from the equipment, and by Sunday night moved to a regular room, which was a blessing!

"Shaman has both demonstrated Medical Intuitive abilities, and, profound healing abilities. She has listened and also given very loving but solid Guidance for me in our sessions. Infused with love and intuitiveness, she has made her way in Northern Minnesota offering massage therapy, caring- healing, listening- empathy, and way more for our community."

Deborah Klejeski

"*Shaman is powerful, innovative, creative, inspiring, hardworking, and spiritually in tuned with the root causes of the mental, emotional and physiological problems visualize through the third and chakras.*

"*This positive healing when applied will correct the spiritual imbalances, cleanse and strengthen the vital life force of the individual.*

"*Shaman's tireless devotion to wellness, holistic living, and the preservation of Rastafari ancient word sound have devoted freely quality time, in proof reading and editing, various Rastafari ancient's texts and manuscript.*

"*Through Shamanic healing and guidance, the duty will be fulfilled to ensure that the aged be protected, the hungry be fed, the naked clothed the sick be nourished and the infants cared for.*

"*This endeavor will be the platform to usher in the guardians of the faith and thus restore a state of spiritual balance.*"

Ras Flako Tafari

Wisemind Publications

"I have patronized several massage therapists over the years. In fact, I had a regular massage therapist when Shaman entered my life. My husband happened upon her and her young son fresh from California and stuck in the snow. He pulled over to help her and she offered half off a massage in appreciation. From that point forward he was convinced that I needed to visit her. I was perfectly happy with the massage therapist that I had and declined his suggestion. He was so convinced of her talent that he purchased a gift certificate for me to prompt me to at least try her out.

"I used the gift certificate with trepidation and just to appease him. My resistance was completely unfounded after I spent an hour with her. Not only did she give an amazing massage, but she read my body and told me things about myself that I would never have suspected as a result from a mere massage. I will never forget her telling me 'You drink too much soda.' I was shocked that she knew that since I was drinking 5-6 cans of soda a day. I have used gift certificates for other massage therapists, but I always come back to Shaman.

"It has been years since my first interaction with Shaman and so many things have happened in my life. I have experienced so many events of great happiness and those of overwhelming pain. I lost my boyfriend of three years to a tragic accident and I was beyond lost. I went to Shaman to help me find some level of relaxation. She helped show me that he was still with me and he was watching over me.

"Months after that session with Shaman I found out something about my boyfriend that completely devastated me. I went to Shaman *and during our session I told her, 'If Brian comes in during our session, please tell him that what he did completely destroyed me.' She asked me what happened and I told her that he knows.*

"During our session she randomly explained to me that Brian had shown her two very distinct things which would only have been significant to the two of us. I always believed in Shaman's ability, but that moment made me more of a believer than I had ever been before. Not only did she share something that only Brian and I would have known, but she helped me realize that I can truly forgive and find peace. That day I left her with a completely renewed sense of calm, peace and faith in the love that I always knew Brian had for me.

"So many people are skeptical about life beyond and the spirits that watch over us. I am blessed that I know Shaman and that her gift has helped me in more ways than one. I am a true believer and not only does she give the most amazing and relaxing massage, she is the most gifted, intuitive woman I know."

Rhea Lund

"I met Shaman some years back on Facebook, and we are still friends today. We made an instant connection when we realized we shared an interest in things all things Energy related, such as hands-on-healing, tarot, astrology, massages, etc. and how this relates to our holistic health. Shaman has read for me intuitively several times, at a distance, and has always been 'right on target.'

"We keep in touch, and whenever I need clear vision on any particular situation, she has always come through for me.

"Most times she simply appears with the right words, 'stark in their simplicity,' highly insightful and clear in their meaning.

"My reply always is: 'how did you know?' My friend Shaman always knows!"

Antoinette Panton

"I am a disabled Veteran with Stage III kidney disease and bi-lateral A-vascular necrosis of the hips. Both my femoral heads on my femurs have decayed and collapsed into my hip sockets.

"Any movement causes severe pain. I live on 500 mg acetaminophen with 7.5 mg of narcotics.

"I had a one hour session with Shaman. I can walk a lot without my cane and have not taken a pain pill since I met Shaman.

"I am a Mayo Clinic patient, VA ABO New Mexico. New Mexico Orthopedics and VA Minneapolis. No one of these medical facilities have done anything for me except supply me narcotics.

"They all want to put two new hip replacements in me. Because of my kidney disease, doctors say I might have acute kidney failure with surgery."

Dennis E. Wiita

"I am the husband of a woman Shaman has been working with for well over 5 years.

"My wife has been diagnosed with pseudo dementia. She started 'slurring' her words about 9 years ago. At present, she can do nothing on her own and hasn't spoken for about 5 years.

"Shaman has worked with Brenda with both massage and energy. Many times the results are unbelievable.

"Shaman's knowledge blows me away at times. She has gone way out of her way to help us; she even tolerates me calling her with questions, and support for me.

"I do know she puts 100% of herself into everything she does.

"I consider her one of the finest people I have ever met.

"When Shaman works with my wife, she just 'coos' and responds positively. My love and thanks to her."

Dale G. Summerfield

To schedule an appointment for an Intuitive Reading or Wellness Consultation or to take part in the Shaman Apprenticeship Program, please visit:

http://seerawolf.com

www.ingramcontent.com/pod-product-compliance
Lightning Source LLC
LaVergne TN
LVHW092245211224
799682LV00004B/23